RELIGIOUS FREEDOM IN CHINA: POLICY, ADMINISTRATION, AND REGULATION

A RESEARCH HANDBOOK

Kim-Kwong Chan and Eric R. Carlson

Santa Barbara, California
Institute for the Study of American Religion
Hong Kong
Hong Kong Institute for Culture, Commerce and Religion

The paper in this publication meets the minimum requirements of the American National Standard for Information Sciences—Permanence of Paper for Printed Library Materials ANSI Z39.48-1984.

ISBN: 0915051036 (pbk.: alk. paper)

Institute for the Study of American religion
P. O. Box 90709
Santa Barbara, CA 93190-0709
U.S.A.

Hong Kong Institute for Culture, Commerce, and Religion
Harcourt Hours, Rm. 1703
38 Gloucester Road
Wanchi, Hong Kong

Alternative Cataloging-in-Publication Data [Sanford Berman]

Chan, Kim-Kwong.

Religious freedom in China: policy, administration, and regulation; a research handbook. By Kim-Kwong Chan and Eric R. Carlson. Santa Barbara, CA: Institute for the Study of American Religion; Hong Kong: Hong Kong Institute for Culture, Commerce, and Religion, copyright 2005.

PARTIAL CONTENTS: Chinese system of law, policy, and administration over religious affairs. The party. The state. Unregistered organizations and "cults." Folk religions and "feudal superstitions." -China's religious policy: theory and implementation. -Sources. Regulations. Government and party documents, notices, and decisions. Publications (internal). Books and periodical articles in English. Books and periodical articles in Chinese. Internet sources. -APPENDIX: Regulations on religious affairs.

1. Freedom of religion--China. 2. Freedom of religion--China--Research--Sources. 3. Religion and state--China. 4. Religion and state--China--Research--Sources. 4. Cults--China--Government policy. 5. Traditional religion--China--Government policy. I. Title. II. Carlson, Eric R. III. Institute for the Study of American Religion. IV. Hong Kong Institute for Culture, Commerce, and Religion. V. Title: Chinese religious freedom.

CONTENTS

CONTRIBUTORS

Eric R. Carlson is a J.D. candidate at J. Reuben Clark Law School, Brigham Young University, 2005.

Kim-Kwong Chan is the Honorary Research Fellow of the Universities Service Center For China Studies, Chinese University of Hong Kong; Executive Secretary of the Hong Kong Christian Council; and, an appointed Justice of the Peace of the HKSAR Government.

W. Cole Durham, Jr. is the Susa Young Gates University Professor of Law and Director, International Center for Law and Religion Studies, J. Reuben Clark Law School, Brigham Young University; A.B., Harvard College; J.D., Harvard Law School.

Brett G. Scharffs is a Professor of Law, J. Reuben Clark Law School, Brigham Young University; B.S.B.A., M.A., Georgetown University; B. Phil., Oxford University; J.D., Yale Law School.

ACKNOWLEDGMENTS

The authors wish to thank several institutions for their generous research and financial support: the Universities Service Centre for China Studies (中國研究服務中心; www.usc.cuhk.edu.hk), located at the Chinese University of Hong Kong; the International Center for Law and Religion Studies (www.law2.byu.edu/Law&Religion), located at Brigham Young University's J. Reuben Clark Law School in Provo, Utah; and the Institute for the Study of American Religion, located in Santa Barbara, California.

All errors remain solely the responsibility of the authors.

Foreword

Brett G. Scharffs and W. Cole Durham, Jr.

This Research Handbook collects, for the first time in English, laws, regulations, and major policy pronouncements about religion in China. It includes national and regional laws and regulations, as well as government and Communist Party documents, notices and decisions, and important commentary and policy directives, including speeches by Party leaders and government publications on religious affairs. The Handbook also compiles public security-related documents, manuals and publications, and secondary sources including books and journal articles in Chinese and English, as well as Internet sources listing sites relevant to religious affairs in China. This Handbook provides a useful roadmap of the publicly available information about religious affairs in China and should be a valuable resource to students, scholars, and government officials who desire to understand the evolving legal treatment of religious issues and the changing religious landscape in China.

To some extent, Western perceptions of the religious situation in China are stuck in a time warp, based upon policies and realities that existed during the Cultural Revolution, when Mao closed all places of worship and tried to extinguish religion altogether. While there is in the United States and elsewhere in the West quite a deep understanding and appreciation for the dramatic economic changes that have taken place in China over the past twenty-five years, there is less understanding of the ways in which laws and policies governing religion have also undergone significant transformation.

For example, while there are still only five officially recognized religious groups in China (Buddhist, Daoist, Islamic, Catholic, and Protestant), and while there is ongoing concern about foreign domination of Christian religions in China, there has been a dramatic increase in the types and levels of interactions between Christians in China and their foreign counterparts. Ongoing tensions exist between the registered and unregistered churches of a single denomination, and unregistered religious groups, sometimes labeled "evil cults," can become targets for particular government concern.

Over the past twenty-five years, there has been a dramatic growth in religious belief in China. The Chinese government estimates that there are more than 100 million religious believers in China today, a majority of whom are Buddhist.[1] The growth has not been limited to the five officially recognized religious groups, but includes unofficial Buddhist organizations and Protestant "house churches," which meet in small groups in believers' homes. For example, after one hundred years of missionary efforts in China from the 1840s until the establishment of the People's Republic of China in 1949, there were approximately 700,000 Protestants in China. Even with the Communist government's official policy of atheism, and the harsh suppression of religion during the Cultural Revolution, since 1978 there has been a quiet resurgence of Protestantism in China. Official estimates place the number of registered Protestants in China at 15 million, while some church groups estimate that there are more than 50 million

[1] Ye Xiaowen, *China's Religions: Retrospect and Prospect*, China News and Report, October 7, 2002, at 10.

unregistered Protestants.[2] While there are five million registered Catholics, the Vatican estimates that there are another seven million unregistered Catholics.[3] These numbers will come as a surprise to many in the West, who remain under the impression that religion is absolutely suppressed in China.

If context is necessary for understanding any text, nowhere is this more clearly the case than in seeking to understand the relationship between law and religion in the People's Republic of China. Having an understanding of the context in which the materials compiled in this Handbook have been written and are interpreted is essential to understanding them. There are many dimensions to the relevant context, and in the remainder of this Foreword we will focus on three: 1) the historical relationship between religion and the state in China; 2) the changing role of law in China; and 3) the international legal framework.

History

During their two-thousand-year history, the imperial governments of China sought supremacy over, and have claimed a divine mandate for, governance and oversight of religion. The last imperial dynasties, the Ming Dynasty (1368–1644) and the Qing Dynasty (1644–1912), each viewed itself as a bridge between heaven and earth, so it was natural for these governments to view themselves as overseers and custodians of all religious groups. In the dynastic ministerial system it was taken for granted that religion was to be monitored and controlled in the service of state ends.

1840–1912

By the nineteenth century, the Qing dynasty was "paralyzed by greed, ignorance and incompetence."[4] Although the Qing dynasty pursued policies of isolationism, European powers sought greater access to Chinese markets. England sought to expand trade with China, in particular by importing opium from India to China. When the Chinese resisted by destroying opium stocks in the southern port city of Guangzhou, the result was the Opium War of 1839–42. As described by Professor Daniel Chow, "The antiquated and ill-equipped armies of the Qing were no match for the superior technology of the British gunboats. After a series of humiliating defeats, China capitulated in the unequal Treaty of Nanjing in 1842."[5]

In the historiography of contemporary China, the period between the end of the Opium War in 1842 and the establishment of the People's Republic in 1949, is viewed as a period of national humiliation and foreign domination, symbolized by the Treaty of Nanjing and the Treaties at Tianjin in 1858.[6] Among other provisions, these treaties

---

[2] See *Religious Freedom in the World: A Global Report on Freedom and Persecution* 102–03 (Paul Marshall ed., 2000).

[3] *Id.*

[4] Daniel C.K. Chow, *The Legal System of the People's Republic of China* 4 (2002).

[5] *Id.* at 5.

[6] *See id.* Chow writes: "A second war with the French and British resulted in a new set of unequal treaties at Tianjin in 1858, and a punitive Anglo-French expedition in 1860 resulted in the occupation of Beijing to

exempted foreigners in more than eighty port cities from Chinese law, subjecting them instead to foreign consular jurisdiction under their own national law.[7]

During this period, Protestant and Catholic churches engaged in extensive missionary work in China, which was closely identified with their sponsoring foreign governments. According to Ye Xiaowen, Consultant to the Chinese Association of Religious Studies, in an article widely disseminated in English, "China entered the 20th century with a deep sense of national humiliation. . . . At this time of national disaster and intensified clashes between indigenous and Western cultures and as the traditional Chinese religions struggled for survival, Protestantism and Catholicism made large-scale inroads into China. A religion that was supposed to spread the words of the Gospel had become the tool of the aggressors."[8]

A series of domestic rebellions in the mid-nineteenth century, including the Taiping, Nian, Muslim, and smaller rebellions, weakened the Qing dynasty. But it was conflicts with foreign powers that were the most damaging to the Qing dynasty, including the Sino-Japanese War of 1894–95.[9] This war was followed almost immediately by the Boxer Rebellion of 1898–1901, in many ways a religiously based uprising fueled by a fanatical hatred of foreigners. Several hundred foreigners were killed before the Boxer Rebellion was crushed by an alliance of eight national armies.[10] In the early twentieth century, revolutionary forces led by Dr. Sun Yat-sen and his Nationalist Party began to plot the overthrow of the Qing dynasty. In 1911 an uprising in Wuhan triggered a series of provincial defections that resulted in the Qing emperor abdicating in 1912.

1912–1949

From 1912–1949, the Nationalist Party attempted but failed to set up a parliamentary system for the fledgling republic. The Nationalists, led by Dr. Sun's successor, Chiang Kai-shek, engaged in a decade-long battle against various warlords, culminating in the Northern Expedition in 1927, "a military campaign led by Chiang that

---

secure the final acceptance by China of the unequal treaty system that lasted for more than a century from 1842 to 1949." *Id.*

[7] *Id.*

[8] Ye, *supra* note 1, at 3.

[9] Chow, *supra* note 4, at 6. Chow explains:

> Under the pretext of intervening in Korea to quell Korean rebels, Japan's modern navy crushed the antiquated Chinese fleet. Forced to pay a huge indemnity as the price of defeat, China funded the indemnity payments by going into debt with European bondholders. The increasing debt to Europe and Japan expanded their spheres of influence in China. By the end of the nineteenth century, Britain, France, Germany, Russia, and Japan all held control over a major naval port and over railways leading to mines in China's interior.

Id.

[10] See Chow, *supra* note 4, at 7. Chow reports: "To punish China, the alliance of foreign nations imposed the draconian Boxer Protocol of 1901 on the Qing government. The Protocol required the destruction of some twenty-five Qing forts and the imposition of a crippling $333 million indemnity. The Boxer Protocol further weakened China just as foreign nations seemed prepared to launch an all-out race for imperialist conquest of China." *Id.*

defeated or absorbed warlord forces into the Nationalist government."[11] The Nationalists then turned their attention to battling the Communists, who had collaborated with the Nationalists in the battles with the warlords. This campaign was interrupted in 1931 when Japan seized the northern region of Manchuria, and in 1937 Japan began an all-out invasion to conquer China. The Nationalists and Communists created a temporary truce while China battled the Japanese in a war that lasted from 1937 to 1945, in which as many as 25 million Chinese lives were lost.

After World War II, all-out conflict erupted between the Nationalists and Communists, now under the leadership of Mao Zedong, and China was once again plunged into war. Although the Nationalists had the backing of the United States, the Communists eventually emerged victorious, and the Nationalists fled to the province of Taiwan where Chiang set up a government in exile. In 1949, Mao formally declared the founding of the People's Republic of China.

1950–1978

After the establishment of the People's Republic of China in 1949, atheism became the official policy of the Communist Party and the State. According to Wang Zuo'an, "Only after the establishment of the People's Republic of China, when the Chinese nation became truly independent, were the Chinese Protestant and Catholic churches able to detach themselves from foreign control and the Chinese believers to manage their own affairs."[12] Five religions were officially recognized, each of which was under the control of the Communist party, and were directed to "eliminate from their ranks remnants and influence of imperialism. . . ."[13] Article 36 of China's constitution states that "religious communities and religious affairs should not be subject to foreign influence."[14]

In 1956–57 there was a period known as the Hundred Flowers Campaign, in which Mao encouraged party members and other intellectuals to voice criticism of the Party. Stung by the severity of the attacks, Mao introduced a series of disastrous political reforms, including the Anti-Rightist Campaign of 1957–58, in which there was a backlash of purification and political revenge against those who had spoken out during the Hundred Flowers Campaign, the Great Leap Forward of 1958–1960, which was an ambitious effort at centralized economic reform that led to a famine killing between 20 and 30 million people, and the Cultural Revolution from 1966–1976, during which Mao consolidated political power by mobilizing teenage Red Guards to inflict political punishment on intellectuals and anyone who opposed Mao. According to Professor Chow, "Combined with the depredations caused by the Anti-Rightist Campaign and the Great Leap Forward, China staggered through a wasted twenty-year period in which the nation

---

[11] Chow, *supra* note 4, at 10.

[12] Wang Zuo'an, *China's Policy on Freedom of Religious Belief.* Wang adds: "[The churches] affirm the 'Principle of the Three 'Self's' (self-administration, self-support, and self-propagation of the gospel) and lead the believers to establish truly self-administered religious enterprises." *Id.*

[13] Ye, *supra* note 1, at 5.

[14] See PRC CONST. art 36.

made no progress in economic, cultural, or spiritual development, but instead suffered needless setbacks and destruction in all of these vital areas."[15]

During this twenty-year period, there were harsh crack downs upon religious leaders and believers, and "Mao closed all places of worship and tried to extinguish religion altogether."[16] The Cultural Revolution ended with Mao's death in 1976, and after a period of political infighting in 1978, Deng Xiaoping emerged as China's new leader. Deng soon began to initiate a series of economic and other reforms that launched China on a path towards modernization.

1978–Present

China's policy and practice with respect to religious affairs since the end of the Cultural Revolution is described in some detail in the Introduction to this Handbook, so we will not add much here, except to note that these policies have been more tolerant of religious belief and believers. In 1978, the Communist Party announced that its focus would change from class struggle to economic development. Over time, some free markets have been allowed to develop, although in keeping with Marxist-Leninist ideology, the state continues to own all real property and the means of production.[17]

In the years since 1978, the five state-registered religions have been given increased latitude to operate under the oversight of the Religious Affairs Bureau, which is controlled by the United Front Work Department, which is itself controlled by the Central Committee of the Communist Party. The last twenty-five years has also seen a surge in activity by unregistered religious groups, and a series of government responses against such groups.[18] Wang Zuo'an, Deputy Director-General of the State Administration for Religious Affairs, has stated, "For an atheistic ruling party to handle religious affairs is a historic task, and a challenge of the party's capability in both leadership and governance."[19] While embracing and advocating atheism, the Communist party has a stated policy of freedom of religious belief. According to Deputy Director Wang, "The freedom of religious belief is a basic right that China's Constitution bestows on her citizens. It is also the basic policy of China's Communist Party on religion."[20]

Deputy Director-General Wang notes that today there are more than 100 million believers in various religions in China. He states, "If the Chinese Communist Party were to impose its atheism on everyone and persecute religious believers, that would only serve to drive 100 million people to an antagonistic position. Such hypothetical practice, which would virtually undermine its very own foundation of governance, is unimaginable." [21] According to Ye Xiaowen, Director-General of the State

---

[15] CHOW, *supra* note 4, at 17.
[16] *Religious Freedom in the World*, *supra* note 2, at 101.
[17] CHOW, *supra* note 4, at 27.
[18] *See Religious Freedom in the* World, *supra* note 2, at 101. In 1991 the government issued Document 6, which called for a checking of unregistered religious groups, and in 1994 the government issued Decrees 144 and 145, mandating the registration of religious groups. In 1999, the government promulgated a new anticult provision of the criminal code, which was used "to impose long prison sentences on leaders of the Falun Gong and Zhong spiritual movements as well as Protestant house church leaders." *Id.*
[19] Wang, *supra* note 12, at 1.
[20] *Id.*
[21] *Id.* at 2.

Administration for Religious Affairs, there has been an evolution of China's religious policies over the past fifty years. But, as Ye maintains, "[T]wo key policies remain constant—that of respect for freedom of religious belief and that of independent running of religious affairs."[22]

In July 2001, the International Olympic Committee selected Beijing to host the 2008 Summer Olympics, and in November 2001, China was granted full membership in the World Trade Organization. While the first event is primarily of symbolic significance, it represents an important victory for the Communist Party only a little more than a decade after the events of Tiananmen Square. Accession to the WTO marks for China an increased commitment to the rule of law in commercial matters, and it may also indicate an increased importance for the role of law in other areas, including religious freedom.

Law and the State

For most of its history (221 BC – 1912 AD), Imperial China did not have a concept of the rule of law that paralleled the western idea of the rule of law. Rather, Confucianism, with its emphasis on hierarchical filial relationships, was the dominant paradigm for understanding the relationship between law and the state. Chow notes that "[w]ithin family and society, all key relationships were those of superior to inferior with a general duty of obedience owed by the inferior to the superior and a reciprocal duty of caring, support, and guidance owed by the superior to the inferior."[23]

Article 36 of China's Constitution states, "Citizens of the People's Republic of China enjoy freedom of religious belief. No state organ, public organization or individual may compel citizens to believe in, or not to believe in, any religion; nor may they discriminate against citizens who believe in, or do not believe in, any religion. The State protects normal religious activities."[24] The Constitution does not define what constitutes a "normal" religious activity.

In a widely distributed statement of China's policy towards religion, in 2002 Ye Xiaowen stated, "In China, the state treats all religions equally and the law protects the equal rights of all religions. While stressing the protection of the freedom to believe in religions, the law also provides for protection of the freedom not to believe in religions. While stressing the protection of the freedom to believe in religions, the law also provides for protection of the freedom not to believe in religions. All are equal before the law. Citizens enjoy the right to religious freedom."[25] This statement would seem to be significantly different from many outsiders' views about the status of religious freedom in China.

There are several keys to understanding Mr. Ye's assertions. First, as noted above, there are only five "religions" recognized in China – Buddhism, Taoism, Islam, Catholicism, and Protestantism – and there is an official, recognized structure for these religions. Every other church or religion is not considered a "religion," but could be considered an "evil cult" that is not entitled to legal recognition or protection. Second, the

---

[22] Ye, *supra* note 1, at 1.
[23] Chow, *supra* note 4, at 43.
[24] *See* PRC CONST. art 36.
[25] Ye, *supra* note 1, at 9.

five recognized "religions" are independent of their foreign counterpart organizations and subject to a degree of oversight and supervision by the Communist Party. Thus, so-called "unregistered" or "underground" churches are not considered to be religions at all, and equal treatment and equal rights apply only to the five officially recognized religious groups.

International Legal Framework

China's location within a broader international system of law is in the process of significant transformation, most prominently influenced by the dramatic increase in foreign trade and rapid economic development in China over the past twenty-five years. This development is most clearly illustrated by China's accession to the World Trade Organization. According to Ye, "With continued economic globalization and WTO membership, China will open wider to the outside world, and so will its religions."[26]

Wang Zuo'an has stated that on the one hand China's policy on religion "reflects the common consensus with regard to religious issues among international community, and on the other hand, it embraces China's own characteristics."[27] According to Ye, China is "ready to join the international community in safeguarding the religion-related human rights."[28] One of the questions for the years ahead is how well China can translate these statements into practice.

The starting point for an analysis of international legal norms governing the right to freedom of religion or belief is article 18 of the Universal Declaration of Human Rights, which virtually all other international instruments parallel: "Everyone has the right to freedom of thought, conscience and religion; this right includes freedom to change his religion or belief, and freedom, either alone or in community with others and in public or private, to manifest his religion or belief in teaching, practice, worship and observance."[29] Several key terms in this provision have particular significance for the freedom of religion or belief.

"Everyone"

All human beings have this right, and it is not limited in its availability to citizens or even permanent residents. Nonresident aliens and stateless persons have the right to freedom of religion or belief. So do foreign religious leaders, religious personnel, and missionaries. Human beings do not lose their rights by taking on religious roles. A recurring problem around the world is the establishment of laws that compromise the scope of religious freedom rights by limiting them to citizens or permanent residents. States may have grounds for keeping certain classes of persons from entering their country (e.g., persons who are likely to be dangerous), but these classifications should not be structured in a way that discriminates on the basis of religion alone.

---

[26] Ye, *supra* note 1, at 12.
[27] Wang, *supra* note 12, at 1.
[28] Ye, *supra* note 1, at 12.
[29] Universal Declaration of Human Rights, Dec. 10, 1948, G.A. Res. 217A(III).

"Has"

Religious freedom is not something bestowed by the state or its statutory regimes, but is something that individuals and religious groups have simply by virtue of their human nature. The point of identifying freedom of religion or belief as a human right is that the right does not depend for its normative legitimacy on how it is factually structured by a state.

"Religion"

If only favored religious groups are included within the definition of "religion," then this may result in discrimination by definitional fiat. Religion and a variety of other terms that may become relevant in applying norms governing freedom of religion or belief (e.g., conscience, belief, sect, clergy, confession, and countless others) are notoriously difficult to define. This is in part because what counts as religion or religious is inherently vague, and the variation in the range of phenomena potentially described by these terms is so vast. But it is also in part because insensitive definitions by the state may themselves be inherently discriminatory and may have the practical effect of imposing limitations on beliefs that individuals and groups sincerely believe to be religious. While these definitional problems may be ultimately insolvable at the level of theory, in the overwhelming majority of cases they are relatively easy to resolve in fact. The approach promulgated by the UN Human Rights Committee in its General Comment No. 22 in 1993 on Article 18, the religious freedom provision of the International Covenant on Civil and Political Rights, provides practical guidance. Paragraph 2 of that document provides, "Article 18 protects theistic, non-theistic and atheistic beliefs, as well as the right not to profess any religion or belief. The terms belief and religion are to be broadly construed. Article 18 is not limited in its application to traditional religions or to religions and beliefs with institutional characteristics or practices analogous to those of traditional religions. The Committee therefore views with concern any tendency to discriminate against any religion or belief for any reasons, including the fact that they are newly established, or represent religious minorities that may be the subject of hostility by a predominant religious community."[30] Many countries are too specific in their legal definitions of religion. In China, for example, even many traditional religions are excluded from the definition of religion. It should be clear that the term "religion" as used in the international instruments includes minority religious groups, as well as groups that are disparaged by referring to them as "sects" or "cults." Any claim that "sects" or "cults" are not "religions" for purposes of asserting religious freedom claims adds injury to insult. It is important to note that just because a group is included within the category of religion, it does not mean that every religious claim it asserts will automatically be vindicated. Extreme claims that threaten others with imminent and palpable injury will clearly justify state intervention under the limitation clause of Article 18 . More generally, religious claims may be subjected to limitations in the narrowly described situations articulated in

[30] Human Rights Committee General Comment 22 (1993) on ICCPR article 18, 20 July 1993, 48th session, U.N. Doc. CCPR/C/21/Rev.1/Add.4 (1993), reprinted in U.N. Doc. HRI/GEN/1/Rev.1 at 35 (1994), para. 2. This General Comment is in effect the official interpretation of Article 18.

the relevant limitations clause. But what occurs in such situations is justifiable state intervention that overrides a religious freedom claim, not state regulation of nonreligious conduct.

"In Community With Others"

A particularly important aspect of freedom of religion or belief is that it protects activities that have a social or communal dimension. While it may be possible to imagine freedom of religion or belief that is limited to the individual, real religious life almost invariably involves interactive conduct in community with others. Thus, religious association laws create legal frameworks that are vital for a host of practical reasons to unimpaired practice and observance of one's religion. In countries committed to religious freedom, such laws aim primarily at facilitating rather than controlling religious organizations.

"Manifestation"

Freedom of religion or belief includes the freedom to manifest one's religion in "teaching, practice, worship and observance."[31] These terms appear to describe in an expansive way general types of conduct embraced within the general category of religious activity. They should be viewed as being representative, and not necessarily exhaustive. As noted by Professor Carolyn Evans, "The United Nations material . . . indicates that the words were used to try to cover a wide range of manifestations of religions and beliefs and were not intended to be read in a limited manner. . . . [I]t may be safely assumed that the intention was to embrace all possible manifestations of religion or belief with the terms 'teaching, practice, worship and observance.'"[32] The terms emphasize that freedom of religion or belief goes beyond holding an "internal" belief to engaging in "external" conduct.

Conclusion

The topic of law and religion in China will remain an issue of tremendous importance in the foreseeable future. This book should provide a valuable resource to those seeking access to information, much of which has heretofore been difficult to obtain.

---

[31] International Covenant on Civil and Political Rights, art. 18(1).
[32] Carolyn Evans, *Freedom of Religion Under the European Convention on Human Rights* (2001).

INTRODUCTION

Mr. Ye Xiaowen, the Director-General of the State Administration on Religious Affairs of the People's Republic of China, wrote in 2002: "Many of you are interested in the evolution of China's religious policies over the past fifty years."[1] As China has undergone tremendous social, economic, and political changes since the early 1980s, its religious freedom policies have followed. Being a signatory of both the Universal Declaration of Human Rights and the International Covenant on Civil and Political Rights, China would also need to be, in principle, accountable to international standards on religious freedom. Mr. Ye's statement echoes the desires and sentiments of many Western scholars who try to comprehend the changing religious situation in China but are limited in their access to the vast amount of material that is scattered in different locations.

Often scholars in the West depend on sporadic media reports with seemingly contradictory indications regarding religious freedom in China. Many of the interpretations are based on sensational reports from particular regions that are then generalized. This Handbook attempts to provide a roadmap of the publicly available sources and materials related to religious policy in China so that Western scholars can have a more comprehensive understanding of the changing religious scene.

Currently, most of these materials are available either on the Internet or in printed form, but are not necessarily readily available in one place. Many of these materials were published in limited printings and are not easy to acquire from ordinary bookstores. This Handbook also describes those organizations within the government that deal with religious affairs and analyzes the often complex bureaucratic interplay in China that affects religious administration. As scholars become aware of the availability of these materials and appreciate the complexity of Chinese governmental and administrative relationships, they can then have a firmer basis to make authoritative interpretations regarding the religious situation in China.

Similarly, the Chinese government also publishes "internal" materials intended for restricted readerships. Legally speaking, such publications are not allowed to circulate outside of the approved readership and certainly not allowed to be made public or to be distributed outside of China. Nevertheless, many of these "internal" publications have found their way into libraries of major universities in the United States, the United Kingdom, Australia, and Hong Kong. This Handbook lists some of these internal documents that are publicly available to bona fide scholars at major universities outside of mainland China. The authors of this Handbook do not encourage scholars to secure these "internal" materials from China or from their Chinese friends or colleagues, for such actions would violate Chinese law. Rather, those documents listed in this Handbook are readily available at major university libraries known to scholars of China.

---

[1] Ye Xiaowen, "China's Religions: Retrospect and Prospect," in *China News and Report*, special issue (7 October 2002), 1.

While several notable works on religious freedom policies and laws have been done in Eastern Europe and the former Soviet Union,[2] relatively little scholarship has been done in English related to religious freedom policies and laws in China.[3]

There are several reasons for this gap. First, the scholarship that has been done in English has tended to focus more on the laws and regulations themselves rather than the context in which they function. Crucially important to understanding are the Party policy papers (the interpretive documents that undergird the regulations) and the complex administrative structures through which the policies are implemented. At this stage, China is still a "rule by law" rather than a "rule of law" society. Second, existing scholarship in English has mainly been limited to analyzing available sources in English. Many of the important policy and interpretive documents—and most of the regulations—have as yet not been translated into English. This paucity of English-language materials presents an almost insurmountable challenge for the scholar who does not know Chinese, complicated by the difficulty in finding and obtaining Chinese sources—even in China. Presses with a very limited network of distribution often print materials on religious affairs and policies; these materials are prepared primarily for religious affairs cadres but not circulated generally among the general public. Third, what documents have been translated mainly have been done by human rights advocacy groups and religious (mainly Christian) groups interested in proselytizing in China. These translations cover a very limited range of the extant regulations.[4] Finally, the Chinese authorities' notion of religion and religious liberty is different than what is preserved in the West. What may be regarded in the West as a legitimate religion may be defined in China by the Chinese authorities as an evil cult and therefore prosecuted as criminal activity, or regarded as an unofficially recognized religion that therefore does not necessary enjoy the right of religious freedom that such a religion would have enjoyed in other countries. Therefore, scholars must look beyond the literal wording of religious regulations in China and broadly examine the whole range of government policies and administration regarding religion and religious activities in order to have a relevant interpretation on religious situations in China.

This Handbook is an effort to summarize the publicly available sources in English and Chinese to enable researchers to build upon previous works and interpret the religious situation in China in its proper context. This Handbook is divided into three sections: (1) a brief overview of law, policy, and administration; (2) the theory and implementation of China's religion policy; and (3) primary and secondary sources.

---

[2] *See, e.g.*, Silvio Ferrari et al. eds., *Law and Religion in Post-Communist Europe* (Peeters Publishing, 2003); "Soul Wars: The Problem of Proselytism in Russia," 12 *Emory International Law Review* 1 (1998).

[3] "China" in this document will refer to the mainland portion of the People's Republic of China (PRC). The laws and policies affecting religious freedom in Hong Kong SAR, Macau SAR, and Taiwan are outside the scope of this Handbook.

[4] Recent issues of the periodical *Chinese Law and Government* have published helpful translations of several important regulations and policy documents. *See* vol. 32, no. 5 (Sep/Oct 1999); vol. 32, no. 6 (Nov/Dec 1999); vol. 33, no. 2 (Mar/Apr 2000); vol. 33, no. 3 (May/Jun 2000); vol. 33, no. 6 (Nov/Dec 2000); vol. 36, no. 2 (Mar/Apr 2003); vol. 36, no. 3 (May/Jun 2003). Several law firms and other legal organizations regularly translate important laws and regulations into English, but since most of their clientele is business-oriented, they have not focused on translating documents related to religion or religious freedom.

SECTION ONE: THE CHINESE SYSTEM OF LAW, POLICY, AND ADMINISTRATION OVER RELIGIOUS AFFAIRS

While law and politics are never completely divorced, in most jurisdictions they enjoy a tense separation. In China, however, law and politics enjoy a close, marriage-like relationship.[1] The Communist Party of China (hereinafter referred to as "the Party" or "CPC") remains the de facto "law" in nearly every sense of the word.[2] In approaching the Chinese situation, the speeches, writings, and theories of the uppermost officials in the Party and government assume a vastly more important role in interpreting the "law" in China than legislation, regulations, or court rulings.[3] In this respect, China's legal system differs dramatically from common law and civil law systems, and even from other socialist law systems. Administrative regulations comprise most of the black-letter "law."[4] Relatively little religiously oriented legislation has been passed by people's congresses on national and regional levels. The will of high Party and government officials often determine the final outcome of regulations, legislation, and—in important cases—court rulings.[5] Thus, while China attempts to move to become a rule-of-law society, in its current status as a one-party state, "law" in all three situations echoes what the Party has previously articulated as policy.

In some countries such as the United States, the law has been designed primarily to protect religion from state interference. In China, however, the opposite appears true, that is, the "law" has been developed to protect the state from interference by religions in civil and governmental affairs. It accomplishes this task by containing religion within defined parameters; religion is considered a private affair that should have no influence in public matters. Citizens in China enjoy a great deal of freedom relative to of religious *belief* but experience considerable limitations on freedom of religious *expression*. Religion is seen as a personal, private matter to be observed in designated venues, primarily the home and designated religious venues (churches, temples, monasteries, etc.). Further, the Chinese constitution states: "No one may make use of religion to engage in

---

[1] The system is described in Chinese as 政法系统, or political-legal system. *See* Ronald C. Keith and Zhiqiu Lin, "The '*Falun Gong* Problem': Politics and the Struggle for the Rule of Law in China," *The China Quarterly* 175 (September 2003): 623–42.

[2] Some scholars describe the current status as "the rule of law with Chinese characteristics." *See* Beatrice Leung, "Religious Freedom and the Constitution in the People's Republic of China: Interpretation and Implementation," *DISKUS* 3:1 (1995), 1–18.

[3] *See* Daniel Chow, *The Legal System of the People's Republic of China*, West Publishers, 2003; James C.F. Wang, "China's Political Framework," in Role H.W. Theen & Frank Wilson, *Comparative Politics: An Introduction to Seven Countries*, second edition, (Prentice Hall, 1992), 496–98; Ronald C. Keith and Zhiqiu Lin, "The '*Falun Gong* Problem': Politics and the Struggle for the Rule of Law in China," *The China Quarterly* 175 (September 2003), 623–42.

[4] R. Lanier Britsch, "The Current Legal Status of Christianity in China," 1995 *BYU Law Review* (1995), 347.

[5] Under Article 128 of the constitution, People's Courts at national and regional levels are responsible to their corresponding People's Congresses, precluding full judicial autonomy.

activities that disrupt public order, impair the health of citizens or interfere with the educational system of the state."[6] Thus, religion should not openly influence civil institutions such as education, health, or marriage. For example, there should be no religious discrimination in marriage: a Muslim should be able to marry a non-Muslim without community interference. Religious organizations cannot run educational institutions such as public schools, and any form of religious instruction is not permitted in any public school.

Aside from general rule-of-law principles, administrative and bureaucratic interests complicate matters in China. Many different government departments and ministries may have assigned tasks relative to the regulation of religious issues, and each organization has a different—sometimes conflicting—role vis-à-vis the legal system. Therefore, one must understand the complex political-administrative dynamic among various bodies at a national and regional level to comprehend the nature of religious administration in a particular part of China. The following sections provide an overview of the administration of religious affairs in China: The Party, The State (including governmental organs and the People's Liberation Army), Religious Associations, and Administrative Divisions.

THE PARTY

The Communist Party of China is the largest political party in the world and currently claims more than 65 million members.[7] While the state constitution is theoretically supreme to other organizations or political parties,[8] the Communist Party of China—the sole ruling party in power in China—still provides the leadership in establishing policy, interpreting law, and enforcing regulations for the country.[9] The Party has, among other powers, the authority to change the state constitution, as has been demonstrated by the recent cases of amending the constitution in accord with current Party theories and including these the constitution.[10] Therefore, the de facto locus of decision making in China lies in the Party, not the government. The Party holds Party Congresses once every few years. The Political Bureau (Politburo) has twenty to twenty-

---

[6] Constitution of the People's Republic of China (1982), Article 36; see also *Freedom of Religious Belief in China*, (Beijing: Information Office of the State Council of the People's Republic of China, 1997); Wang Zuo'an, "China's Policy on Freedom of Religious Belief," paper presented at the 10th Annual International Law and Religion Symposium, 5–8 October 2003, Provo, Utah, USA.

[7] For an official description of the CPC, see http://www.china.org.cn/english/Political/26151.htm.

[8] Constitution of the People's Republic of China (1982), Article 5.

[9] In fact, the constitution enshrines the CPC as the exclusive political Party to lead the country. *Id.* Preamble. Also, Peng Zhen, vice-chair of the Committee to Revise the Constitution, noted in 1980: "the Party leads the people in enacting the law and leads the people in observing the law" (党领导人民制定法律,也领导人民遵守法律). Peng Zhen, "On the Work of the Standing Committees of Local People's Congresses," 18 April 1980.

[10] At the Third Central Committee meeting of the Sixteenth Party Congress (11–14 October 2003), the Party recommended amending the constitution by adding the current "Three Represents" theory into the Party constitution. *See* http://www.china.org.cn/chinese/zhuanti/sljszqh/421625.htm. The National People's Congress passed a resolution in March 2004 to incorporate the "Three Represents" theory into the state constitution.

five members and is selected from the CPC Central Committee (about 200 members), which is in turn elected by the delegates at the Party's Congress. A small group of leaders, the Standing Committee of the Political Bureau (中央政治局常委), are the most powerful. These men (currently nine) outline policy goals and plans. Top Party leaders almost always hold parallel positions in the state government as well.

The CPC is divided into a number of departments including the Organization Department, Military Commission, and Disciplinary and Inspectorate Commission, etc. One of these divisions is the United Front Work Department (UFWD, 中央统战部), which coordinates different sectors of the population, including religious groups, to support the Party and unify the country. The UFWD originally sought to include those who did not oppose the CPC in modernization and economic liberalization, rather than focusing on ideology. The UFWD works with overseas Chinese, intellectuals, minorities, and artists, as well as religious believers. Eventually, the UFWD was entrusted with formulating the Party's policy on religion, aiming to rally the support of religious believers around common political objectives—that is, support for the Party. The UFWD units of the local CPC branch would also oversee and implement the Party policy on religion through both Party organs and the government's administrative apparatus.[11] The UFWD also interprets religious policies. In locales where no specific governing unit on religious affairs exists, the local UFWD often assumes the role of religious administrator.

Atheism enjoys a privileged position in China. According to the Party constitution, a Party member should believe in Marxist-Leninist-Mao Zedong Thought. In theory, then, a Party member should be an atheist. Normally, if a Party member were found to believe in religion, s/he would be dismissed from the Party. Although the state constitution guarantees citizens the right to believe in religion, that right does not extend into internal Party affairs. Average Han Chinese Party members cannot normally enjoy religious freedom and Party membership simultaneously; however, exceptions are made for Party members from one of the designated national minority groups (discussed more fully below). In this respect, the Party constitution trumps the state constitution in religious matters.

It is widely known that some Han Party members are religious believers. So long as these members do not publicize their religiosity, such as openly denouncing atheism or publicly receiving initiation rites involved in joining a religious group, many of the Party branches tolerate such a situation. It is also reported that the Party in several cases has refused to grant Party withdrawal applications from members who had openly declared their religious allegiance, for it may reduce Party prestige and membership numbers. Therefore, Party members who embrace religion may still be on the active roll-call list of the Party yet at the same time be semi-publicly engaged in religious life.[12]

---

[11] Chan Kim-Kwong and Alan Hunter, "New Light on Religious Policy in the PRC," *Issues and Studies* 31 (Feb 1995), 23.

[12] One of the authors (Chan) has witnessed many such cases in China, especially in Christian circles. In some extreme cases an elder of the local Christian community is even secretary of the local village Party branch. As for the Buddhist and Daoist groups, there is no strict membership requirement and therefore a "dual-membership" situation is not relevant. Since the Muslims in China are identified with national minority groups, there is no strict enforcement of Party rule over its members of national minority background regarding religious issues.

THE STATE

Constitution

The 1982 state constitution is theoretically the supreme document undergirding China's legal and governmental system. Promulgated by the National People's Congress, it sets forth the legal relationships between the government and the people, and in that process recognizes the existence of religion. Chapter II lists "The Fundamental Rights and Duties of Citizens." Therein, Article 36 reads:

> Citizens of the People's Republic of China enjoy freedom of religious belief.
> No state organ, public organization or individual may compel citizens to believe in, or not to believe in, any religion; nor may they discriminate against citizens who believe in, or do not believe in, any religion.
> The state protects normal religious activities. No one may make use of religion to engage in activities that disrupt public order, impair the health of citizens or interfere with the educational system of the state.
> Religious bodies and religious affairs are not subject to any foreign domination.[13]

Theoretically, citizens enjoy unlimited freedom of belief or internal freedom of conscience. Further, the constitution protects against compulsion toward belief or nonbelief and protects against discrimination among believers and nonbelievers. In matters of religious practice and expression, however, the state grants itself broad regulatory powers, beginning with extending its protection only to what are considered "normal" religious activities. Religious activities must not disrupt, impair, or interfere with state responsibilities. Finally, foreign domination or interference in religious affairs is prohibited. Citizens generally have not been able to sue based only on rights contained in the constitution, leaving those whose freedom of religious belief have been violated without a remedy. Recently, however, Chinese courts have been more open to the possibility of "judicialization of the Constitution."[14]

National People's Congress

The National People's Congress (NPC, 全国人民代表大会) is on paper China's chief legislative body. However, because it meets only once a year, though, the NPC has yet to mature into a true deliberative body. The Standing Committee and the Presidium issue most of the day-to-day legislation. In the field of religious affairs, a nationwide

[13] Constitution of the People's Republic of China (1982), Article 36.
[14] *See* Qi Yuling v. Chen Xiaoqi Case of Infringement of Citizen's Fundamental Rights of Receiving Education Under the Protection of the Constitution by Means of Infringing Right of Name, 5 *Zuigao Renmin Fayuan Gongbao* [Gazette of the Supreme People's Court of the People's Republic of China] 158 (2001); Chris X. Lin, "A Quiet Revolution: An Overview of China's Judicial Reform," 4 *Asian Pacific Law and Policy Journal* 180, 192–205 (2003).

"Religious Affairs Law," holding more force than administrative regulations, was proposed in the late 1980s but has not yet been formally considered and passed.[15]

The national legislature has passed various pieces of legislation and resolutions that affect religious affairs. In October 1999, for example, the Standing Committee of the NPC passed a legislative resolution that designated Falungong as an "evil cult," enabling the government to move against it under Article 300 of the PRC Criminal Law.[16] In other words, the NPC has the legislative power to define a religious group as an "evil cult." Once this determination is made, the government can then activate the legal machinery to act relative to the group under Chinese law. There seems to be little, if any, room to challenge a decision of the NPC, for it is the final legislative authority in China. Since there is no constitutional court in China, the general courts (People's Court) in China cannot challenge the constitutionality of legislation issued by the NPC.[17]

Provincial, municipal, and county governments each have people's congresses to pass legislation within their respective jurisdictions. Often religious regulations passed by people's congresses differ from region to region, depending on the local situation and political climate. For example, the religious affairs regulation for Shanghai (1995) contains a clause prohibiting folk religious practices, while Beijing's corresponding regulation (2002) does not.[18] Regulations from Muslim-dominated areas may have special provisions catering to Islamic concerns, such as the running of Quranic schools for children.[19]

State Council

The State Council (国务院) of the PRC is the highest-ranking state body and, at least nominally, wields executive power. Though the National People's Congress is structurally the legislative body, the State Council in reality enacts many regulations that have the force of law in China. The State Council also has power to issue decrees that are

---

[15] *See* Ma Jin, "Discussions of Certain Questions on Legislation of Religious Ordinances," Part One, in *The Questions Of Religion in the World Today*, (Beijing: State Administration of Religious Affairs and Research Center on Religion) (internal document) No. 8, 2003, 14–24; *See* Chan Shun-Hing & Lam Sui-ki, "The Transformation and Development of Church-State Relations in Contemporary China: A Case Study of the Catholic Church," in *Ching Feng: A Journal on Christianity and Chinese Religion and Culture*, vol. 3 (2002), 121.

[16] 全国人民代表大会常务委员会关于取缔邪教组织, 防范和惩 治邪教活动的决定 ("Decision of the Standing Committee of the National People's Congress on Banning Cult Organizations, Guarding Against and Punishing Cult Activities"), 30 October 1999. *See also* James T. Richardson and Bryan Edleman, "Falun Gong and the Law: Development of Legal Social Control in China," *Nova Religio* vol. 6, no. 2 (April 2003), 277–93.

[17] Indeed, under Article 128 of the constitution, People's Courts at national and regional levels are responsible to their corresponding people's congresses, foreclosing any sort of meaningful judicial review. *See also* Daniel Chow, *The Legal System of the People's Republic of China*, West Publishers, 2003.

[18] *See* Article 28 of the *Shanghai Municipal Regulations on Religious Affairs*, issued on 30 November 1995 (see *infra* Section Three for details).

[19] *See* Article 12 of the *Provisional Regulation on the Administration of Religious Affairs in Xinjiang Uygur Autonomous Region*, issued 23 August 1990 (see *infra* Section Three for details).

binding on all government organizations.[20] Further, the State Council supervises the work of dozens of other ministries, bureaus, commissions, and institutions.[21] The following are the ministries or bureaus that have direct and indirect jurisdiction over religious affairs.

State Administration for Religious Affairs / Religious Affairs Bureau

The State Administration for Religious Affairs (SARA,国家宗教事务局[22]) is an "organization directly under the State Council" (国务院直属机构), a level just below a full ministry. While other organizations have influence over religious affairs, SARA is the preeminent organization that affects daily administration over religious affairs. SARA is also empowered to issue binding nationwide regulations.[23] Its official mandate to represent the government in implementing religious policy includes the following:

> to study and propose policies and guidelines for the work related to religious affairs, formulate and implement such policies and guidelines, investigate and study the religious situation in China and abroad to maintain grasp of the developments, study the issue of religious theories, propose policy suggestions; guide and promote religious circles to conduct their activities within the framework of law and policies and protect citizens' freedom of religious belief.[24]

SARA has a Director General,[25] three Deputy Director Generals and is divided into four departments. The General Affairs Office (办公室) is responsible for cadre education, internal management of documents, human resources, internal finance, and coordinating with the Party. The Policy and Regulation Department (政策法规司) researches and drafts regulations and other related materials and propaganda. The Policy and Regulation Department also oversees religious work in China. The First Business Department (业务一司) oversees Buddhism, Daoism, and Islam and works with their respective religious associations (see below) to approve religious leaders and religious publications. The Second Business Department (业务二司) has similar responsibility for the Christian religions (Catholic, Protestant, and Orthodox) and is additionally tasked with ensuring that the Christian religions in China are independent from any foreign

---

[20] *See, e.g.*, Decrees 144 and 145, in *Provisions on the Administration of Religious Activities of Aliens within the Territory of the People's Republic of China, and Regulations on Administration of Sites for Religious Activities* (Beijing: China Legal Press, 1994).

[21] For more information about the State Council and an overview of its structure, see "The State Council," at http://english.peopledaily.com.cn/data/organs/statecouncil.shtml.

[22] The name of this organization is traditionally translated as "State Administration for Religious Affairs," or SARA. But provincial organizations are normally translated as "Religious Affairs Bureaus" (e.g., "the Zhejiang Religious Affairs Bureau"), though the Chinese characters (宗教事务局) are the same for both.

[23] *See, e.g.*, 境内外国人宗教活动管理规定实施细则 (Specific Rules for Implementing the Regulations on the Management of Religious Activities of Foreigners in China) Decree of the State Administration for Religious Affairs No.1, issued 26 September 2000 by Director-General Ye Xiaowen. *See infra* Section Three for more details on this regulation.

[24] "The Organizational Structure of the State Council," at http://www.china.org.cn/english/features/state_structure/64784.htm.

[25] As of this publication, the director-general is Ye Xiaowen (叶小文).

domination, a political reaction from the history of the foreign-dominated past of Christianity in China.[26] At the National Religious Work Conference held in January 2004, it was decided the SARA will establish a new unit under one of these business departments to focus on folk religions.[27]

SARA has several organizations under its umbrella. The Religion Research Center (宗教研究中心) is largely self-explanatory: it undertakes studies of religious theory and practice in China and around the world. Two other organizations are formally separate from SARA but operate in close coordination. The *China Religion* Magazine Press (《中国宗教》杂志社) publishes the monthly magazine of the same name, featuring articles that promote and echo the religious policies of the government and highlights of (sanctioned) religious activities around the country.[28] Occasionally it also reports on the religious situations overseas. The Religion and Culture Press (宗教文化出版社) publishes reference materials on religion, religious laws and regulations, religious policy and theory, religious texts, some religious canonical materials (such as the Quran), and other materials on religion. It also publishes classified bulletins and study materials for internal circulation.

At the provincial level, similarly organized Religious Affairs Bureaus (RABs) exist to oversee religious work. Municipal, county, and even some township/village governments also have Religious Affairs Bureaus or equivalent units. As part of the government's recent downsizing effort, RABs have merged in some locales with National Minority Bureaus to form Nationality and Religious Bureaus (民族宗教局). However, within the merged offices, there are clear administrative divisions between these two groups of cadres. RABs at every level promulgate regulations governing religious affairs in their jurisdiction. RABs also work with religious associations (described below) at the same administrative level. Since nearly all RAB cadres are Party members, they are not religious, for Party membership normally precludes religious belief.[29] While cadres at the national SARA generally have access to detailed knowledge about specific religion and understand nuances among and within religions, many lower-level religious cadres, particularly at the local administrative levels, have little knowledge of religious specifics.[30] A majority of the cases reported by foreign media on abuses of religious freedom in China take place at county levels or below, where low-level cadres often lack professional knowledge on religion and religious policy. This situation is gradually changing as the government attempts to upgrade cadres' professional knowledge in their respective fields.[31] Nowadays, it is not uncommon to encounter younger religious affairs

---

[26] See 国家宗教事务局 (State Administration for Religious Affairs), at http://www.wiseman.com.cn/gcxmavin/gcxorgan/government/03/03016/03016a.htm. This Web site also contains the names of the directors-general of the bureau and its different departments.

[27] Chan, personal communication with a senior staff member of a provincial RAB, February 2004; name and location undisclosed for security reasons.

[28] *See infra* Section Three, "Periodicals in Chinese," for more information on this publication.

[29] Officials in RAB offices are usually not religious believers. The government asserts that religious belief could lead to biases in administration. Some exceptions are made, however, for national minorities, as described *infra*.

[30] For more information about the RAB, see Philip L. Wickeri, *Seeking the Common Ground: Protestant Christianity, the Three-Self Movement, and China's United Front* (1988), 70 et seq.

[31] See Luo Shuze, "Some Hot Issues in Our Work on Religion," *Qiushi*, no. 5 (1996); translated in *Chinese Law and Government* 33, no. 2 (Mar/Apr 2000), 105.

cadres with graduate degree in religious studies. The RABs usually deal only with religions that are officially recognized and registered and hence are not involved in adjudicating cases concerning “evil cults.” SARA and local RABs have no enforcement power.

Public Security Bureau, National Security Bureau, and Ministry of Justice

The Ministry of Public Security (公安部), another organization under the State Council, is responsible for the internal security of China, with responsibilities similar to but broader than the FBI in the United States.[32] The Ministry of Public Security has corresponding Public Security Bureaus (公安局 or 公安厅) at the provincial and local levels. Cadres at Public Security Bureaus (PSBs) usually deal with religious activities that are not officially recognized by authorities, and may have a bearing on social security. Religious groups that are not recognized by the government and those unregistered groups within the officially recognized religions are considered either “illegal groups” or “evil cults” by the authorities. Once a group is considered “illegal,” it is within the PSB’s jurisdiction to enforce the law against these groups, including arrests and detentions. At local levels, PSBs are part of local governments and are subject to local politics. The local PSB may or may not ask local religious groups for a recommendation on the legitimacy of the targeted groups. Often, PSBs do not necessarily consult with RABs when they make arrests on “unregistered” religious groups. PSBs at the provincial level usually have a dedicated unit to monitor suspicious religious groups or activities. A substantial amount of reported abuses on religious believers are related to PSB personnel rather than RAB cadres.[33]

The Ministry of National Security (or National Security Bureau, 国家安全部 or 国安部) is responsible for China’s external intelligence gathering and counterespionage. It monitors, among other things, the activities of foreigners in China, foreign groups that have interests in China, and the activities of overseas Chinese that may influence China. The Ministry itself has assumed a very low profile; its existence was not even publicly acknowledged until the 1990s. Because of China’s concern with foreign religious groups infiltrating into China, this Ministry has the responsibility of monitoring foreigners viewed as likely to engage in proselytizing in China, including foreign language teachers sent by faith-based agencies serving on Chinese campuses. This Ministry is assumed to have a task force that deals specifically with religion.

Although there is no formal provision prohibiting a religious believer to work for the PSB/NSB,[34] potential candidates go through a political background check. Religious believers are usually regarded as politically unreliable, for they do not subscribe to Marxist-Leninist-Mao Zedong Thought. In practice, therefore, officers of the PSB/NSB are not religious believers, except for those from national minority groups. An officer

[32] Note that the Ministry of Public Security usually “outranks” SARA in administrative affairs.

[33] For example, see several recent reports of PSB officers arresting Christians at http://www.china21.org. See also various documents translated in “Religion and Public Security in China: 1999–2002,” *Chinese Law and Government* 36, no. 2 (Mar/Apr 2003).

[34] Indeed, Article 36 of the constitution prohibits discrimination based on religious belief or nonbelief.

who converts to religious belief may face reprimand.[35] The Chinese police force under the PSB has no police chaplaincy.

The Ministry of Justice runs all jails, detention centers, and labor re-education camps. Like the PSB/NSB, this system has no provision for religious activities or any form of chaplaincy services. Chinese authorities operate under the assumption that the Party provides a comprehensive ideology (i.e., scientific materialism) that is effective and sufficient to elevate the moral level of its prisoners as well as the social reformation of a person from a criminal into a model citizen.[36] Other than dietary provisions (e.g., for Muslims), there is no provision for religious activities of the detainees and prisoners. In fact, the policy of freedom of religious belief, as set forth in the constitution, does not usually extend to the staffs of the state law enforcement agencies or to those who are under the jurisdiction of these state organs, such as a labor camp detainees or prisoners.

Nationality / Minority Affairs

China's population includes fifty-six ethnic groups,[37] with Han Chinese comprising approximately 92% of the population.[38] In an estimated 35% of the geographic territory and at least 10% of the population (including Hans living among these national minority groups under the ruling of the autonomous governments), the religious policies are different from what has been in observed in Han-dominated areas. Such religion policies may favor the rights of certain religious groups, or may promote a particular religion, or may even suppress some religious groups.

The government has established the Nationality Affairs Committee (民族事务委员会) under the State Council to oversee national minority affairs in places where there is a significant population of national minority groups.[39] The Committee was established to protect the rights of these minority groups by preserving their cultural heritage and granting these group special socioeconomic privileges to promote their economic and political status in China. The national minority groups are not subject to the strict birth control policies (as the Hans are) and students of the ethnic minorities enjoy a larger university entrance quotas. Areas with high percentages of national minorities can form their own autonomous government that can pass legislation favoring minorities. These policies favoring ethnic minorities extend to all spheres of life, including religion. Many of these groups embrace certain religions as part of their cultural heritage. For example, most Tibetans embrace Buddhism, the Tajiks are nearly all Muslims, and the Olongcuns[40] believe in shamanism.

---

[35] There are documented cases to suggest that such officers face harsh punishment. *See* http://china21.org/simpChinese/news/2003/060203.htm.

[36] *See Regulations on Education Reform Works in Prison*, Ministry of Justice Decree No. 79, effective 1 August 2003, at http://www.southcn.com/news/community/shzt/prison/data/200405111113.htm. . This regulation makes no provision for the religious needs and activities of the inmates.

[37] This official number is constantly challenged from academic circles regarding the definition of an ethic minority group. For instance, the Yi people comprise many subgroups with different languages and customs, which arguably could be considered different groups.

[38] The fifty-five other ethnic groups, however, occupy nearly 60% of China's territory.

[39] This is a full ministry and has corresponding branches at lower administrative levels.

[40] The Olongcuns live in the northern part of Heilongjiang Province, with counterparts living in Siberia.

There are differences regarding the handling of religious affairs between national minorities and Hans, though there has been relatively little research in this field. Differences in administration can be attributed to the policies on national minorities, which often supersede national religious policy. The basic assumption is that religions among the national minorities are regarded as a cultural rather than a religious issue and are under the protection of national minority policies. For example, a national minority can embrace a religion (such as shamanism) that would otherwise be regarded as feudal superstition and banned for Han Chinese. A national minority cadre who practices a religion can still retain his/her position in the Party and the government, although s/he would be discouraged from openly practicing his/her religion. A Han cadre, however, would usually be expelled from the Party and government position were she found to embrace religious belief.

In some extreme situations, the government of a national minority autonomous region could even use legislative means to elevate a certain religion as the dominant one and to suppress other religions—a policy that is contrary to the national policy on religion. The Christians in southern Xinjiang have been living in a legal limbo after the Xinjiang government declared that no religion except Islam exists there. Apparently, officials from the SARA had tried to persuade the Uygur Autonomous Government of Xinjiang to fully implement the national policy on religion at Xinjiang—namely, equal status for religious groups other than Islam—but the Xinjiang government claimed that it had the full power to pass its own legislation and implement its own policy on religion (a policy favoring Islam). In fact, the central government can do little, for any strong intervention by the central government may trigger political backlash from the Uygurs in Xinjiang, possibly precipitating a national security crisis.

Other Ministries Affecting Religious Affairs

In the past, China adopted a Soviet-style planned economy; such an economic system divided the nation into various production sectors under the administration of different ministries. For example, oil fields are under the administration of the Ministry of Petroleum (itself under the State Council) rather than the local civil authorities. The Ministry oversees petroleum production facilities such as Shengli Oilfield in Shandong Province, which employ nearly half-million staff and their dependents. The petroleum industry in China is virtually autonomous, with its own communities, schools, and colleges. Similarly, the Ministry of Forestry has exclusive authority over huge tracts of forestry, with hundreds of villages and township within its jurisdiction. The railway system, too, is an autonomous community with not only its own medical and educational system but also independent telecommunication networks. These ministries and systems have authority to govern their territories and the livelihoods of those who are living under their jurisdiction.

The religious activities within the jurisdiction of these ministries and systems are de jure under the administration of the local governments but de facto under the administrations of these ministries. Hence these areas are often not subject to the laws and regulations legislated by the People's Congresses of the local governments. For example, recently, Christians who reside at the Shengli Oilfield wanted to build a church.

Because Shengli Oilfield is located in Shandong province, the Shandong Religious Affairs Bureau should have jurisdiction over this matter. However, it was the Oilfield Party Committee that decided whether to allow the Christian community to build a church, and the United Front Work Department of the Oilfield Party Committee that oversaw the day-to-day activities of religious believers in the oilfield. Often these ministries may disregard the religious policies and regulations issued by SARA, for these specialized ministries often have an equal or higher ministry status than SARA. Therefore, religious affairs in these huge state-owned enterprises depends more the policies adopted by the leadership of these units than the policies and regulations dictated by SARA or regional RABs.

Judiciary

The Chinese Constitution establishes two sets of judicial bodies: people's courts and procuratorates. The Supreme People's Court supervises the lower courts. Procuratorates are "state organs for legal supervision"[41] and exercise both prosecutorial and supervisory roles, investigating and prosecuting criminal violations and official misconduct.

Article 126 of the constitution asserts the principle of judicial independence.[42] As a quasi–civil law country, however, People's Courts at national and regional levels are responsible to their corresponding People's Congresses,[43] and the National People's Congress is the final arbiter of statutory interpretation.[44] As China attempts to move from "rule by law" (依法治国) to "rule of law" (法治), judicial independence will become increasingly important. China's accession to the WTO has prompted debate as to how to make China's laws consistent with international standards of judicial independence, judicial review, transparency, and human rights.[45] Legal scholars and the judiciary recently have been more receptive to the concept of judicialization of the Constitution, allowing enforcement of constitutionally enshrined rights.[46]

With regard to religious administration, the courts have not played a large role in protecting religious liberties in China. Until the constitution is judicialized, the true scope of "freedom of religious belief" as outlined in Article 36 will remain untested.

---

[41] Constitution of the People's Republic of China (1982), Article 129.

[42] "The people's courts exercise judicial power independently, in accordance with the provisions of the law, and are not subject to interference by any administrative organ, public organization or individual."

[43] Constitution of the People's Republic of China (1982), Article 128. *See also* Young Nam Cho, "Symbiotic Neighbour or Extra-Court Judge? The Supervision over Courts by Chinese Local People's Congresses," *China Quarterly* vol. 176, 1068–1083 (2003).

[44] "The power of legal interpretation belongs to the Standing Committee of the National People's Congress." Legislation Law of the People's Republic of China (2000), Article 42.

[45] The Chinese phrase for making domestic laws conform to international norms is 与国际接轨: "making the (railroad) tracks consistent with the international gauge." Chris X. Lin, "A Quiet Revolution: An Overview of China's Judicial Reform," 4 *Asian Pacific Law and Policy Journal* 180, 181 (2003).

[46] *See* Qi Yuling v. Chen Xiaoqi Case of Infringement of Citizen's Fundamental Rights of Receiving Education Under the Protection of the Constitution by Means of Infringing Right of Name, 5 *Zuigao Renmin Fayuan Gongbao* [Gazette of the Supreme People's Court of the People's Republic of China] 158 (2001); Chris X. Lin, "A Quiet Revolution: An Overview of China's Judicial Reform," 4 *Asian Pacific Law and Policy Journal* 180, 192–205 (2003).

People's Liberation Army

The military forces of China, jointly called the People's Liberation Army (PLA), are comprised of the Army, the Navy, the Air Force, the Second Artillery (Missile), and the Armed Police Force (a professional military force for internal security purposes, such as riot control, border control, and forest firefighting).[47] Since the military forces are the armed branch of the Party and under the command of the Military Committee of the Party,[48] it does not follow the rules and regulations outlined by the State Council. In fact, the PLA has its own rules and policy. Legally speaking, there is no religious discrimination in the *Military Service Law of People's Republic of China* and Chinese religious believers can apply to join the military force in China.[49] However, the PLA does have the *CPLA Interior Service Regulations* that requires all members of the PLA to swear to follow CPC policy.[50] The *Regulations Regarding CPLA Political Works* demands all PLA personnel to embrace Marxist-Leninist Thought and Mao Zedong Thought.[51]

There is no provision allowing any religious activities in the PLA. Therefore, there is no religious activity within the PLA's jurisdiction. In other words, the PLA represents a third exception to Article 36 of the Constitution of China regarding freedom of religious belief. The military forces in China do not have the same right of freedom of religious belief as ordinary citizens, even though many military personnel are not Party members. The PLA is one of the very few major military forces in the world, other than the military forces such as the People's Army of of North Korea, that has no military chaplaincy. Instead, it has political commissars from the Party to play the role of morale officer as the military chaplain does in military forces in other countries. This lack of military chaplaincy may have implications on the right of POWs regarding religious liberty guaranteed in of the *Geneva Convention on Prisoners of War*, of which China is a signatory.[52] For example, a POW taken by the PLA may request a religious service, which PLA could not deliver. Further, a military chaplain of the captive POW has no counterpart in PLA to liaise with in dealing with religious issues.[53]

---

[47] The total number of military personnel is around 3 million (including the Armed Police Force). Additionally, military-run industrial complexes employ several million people, along with their dependents.

[48] In recent years the government created a parallel Military Committee under the State Council to give an impression that the People's Liberation Army is not the Party's military but the state military. Given the fact that China is a one-party state and the committee members of both committees are identical, the PLA is, de facto, under the control of the CPC.

[49] See Article 3 of the *Military Service Law of the People's Republic of China*, effective 1 October 1984.

[50] Article 7 of the *CPLA Interior Service Regulation*, issued by the Military Commission on 26 May 1990.

[51] *Regulations Regarding CPLA Political Work*, issued by the Military Commission on 1 January 1991.

[52] See Geneva Convention Related to the Treatment of Prisoners of War (August 12, 1948), Articles 34–37.

[53] During the Korean War, some U.S. POWs under Chinese captivity were allowed to have religious services conducted by captured missionaries and POW chaplains/officers. It is not known whether the POW chaplains, like medical doctors, were treated under the Geneva Convention not as captive personnel but as camp assistants with latitude of freedom to exercise their duties. Chan, personal correspondence with Ted Baker of The Korean War Project, 4 November 2003. However, other POWs, such as Douglas Tanner, recalled that there was absolutely no allowance for religious activities, even for funeral services for dead prisoners in the camp, during his thirty-three months of POW confinement under the Chinese Army. Chan, personal correspondence with Douglas Tanner, January 9, 2004.

There may be some exceptions if the PLA draws recruits from the national minority groups, as some of these minority groups adopt a religion as part of their ethnic identity (such as Tibetan Buddhists). On a practical level, however, there are PLA members who have embraced religion. On some PLA bases, the local military command tolerates officers (many are influenced by their family members who are religious believers) who subscribe to religion under the following conditions: they do not wear military uniforms to religious venues, such as church buildings, they do not conduct religious activities within the military compound, and they keep a low profile. It seems that Chinese pragmatism and the culture of face-saving prevails over legal restrictions.[54] To this date, there are no documented reports of any PLA members who have been publicly persecuted because of religious faith.

In border provinces, such as Xinjiang, Heilongjiang, or Yunnan, the PLA also establishes Production and Construction Corps. These Corps are under military command and run huge farms, factories, mines, and even trading companies. These Corps were established by the PLA in the 1950s to supply the material needs of the PLA stationed in bordering regions. Later, these Corps evolved into quasi-autonomous governments with huge production capacities and geographic jurisdiction covering vast swaths of land. Anyone working for these Corps farm and factories, including their dependents, is under military command. The policy of freedom of religious belief also does not apply to the populations under the command of these Corps, for the Corp is legally speaking under the jurisdiction of the PLA, even though most of these people are civilians. In recent years, it has been documented that some regiments of these Corps in Xinjiang Province tolerate religious activities among Muslim Corps members because it is a Muslim-dominated area. Such allowance has not yet been extended to other faiths.

Religious Associations and Other Religious Groups

The government has differentiated four categories of religious belief. First, the five recognized religions (Daoism, Buddhism, Islam, Catholicism, and Protestantism) are officially sanctioned as long as they work within the government-registered patriotic religious associations and keep within government-set parameters as dictated by the religious policies. Second, unregistered religious organizations exist in some locations that may have the tacit consent of local government officials or may be banned and under prosecution of the state security organs. In some cases, they are labeled as "evil cults" (see below). Third, "feudal superstitions" and folk religions are officially frowned upon but rarely prosecuted unless the beliefs interfere with public order or safety. Fourth, religions and religious practices ascribed by national minority groups as their cultural heritage are permitted—not under the aegis of religious policy but national minority policy. These religions are tolerated but usually do not spread beyond their ethnic

[54] Chan, personal correspondence with Christian church leaders near a PLA base (location undisclosed due to security reasons), November 2003.

boundaries. This fourth group is described above in the "Nationality / Minority Affairs" section.

Religious Associations

The Chinese government recognizes seven religious associations for its five recognized religions. Islam, Buddhism, and Daoism have one association each.[55] The (government-recognized) Chinese Catholic Church has two associations,[56] and (officially sanctioned) Protestant churches collectively have two.[57] The government's goal in maintaining these organizations is to ensure that religious activities remain within government-set parameters. Thus, these "patriotic" associations carry out their work in close cooperation with the government, and their leaders publicly echo the Party line.[58] Dissenting religious organizations that operate in China are not part of these groups: the Vatican-sanctioned Chinese Catholic Church hierarchy and the unregistered Protestant "house churches" are two examples. The China Christian Council is a member of the World Council of Churches and the Buddhist Association of China is active in the Buddhist World Federation.

Unregistered Organizations and "Cults"

All organizations—including religions—must be registered to be legal. In some locales, unregistered groups with membership greater than three persons are illegal.[59] After the 1989 Tiananmen Square incident, the government began intensifying its oversight and enforcement of the law over many forms of unregistered groups. Unregistered religious groups, which continued to grow through the 1990s, were swept up in periodic law enforcement efforts. In 1995, the State Council and CPC Central Committee issued a circular labeling several Christian groups "evil cults" and making

---

[55] Chinese Islamic Association (中国伊斯兰教协会), Buddhist Association of China (中国佛教协会), and Daoist Association of China (中国道教协会).

[56] There used to be three Catholic organizations in the early 1980s, Chinese Catholic Patriotic Association (中国天主教爱国会), Chinese Catholic Bishops' Conference (中国天主教主教团), and Chinese Catholic Religious Affairs Committee (中国天主教教务委员会). The Chinese Catholic Religious Affairs Committee later merged into the Catholic Bishops' Conference.

[57] Three-Self Patriotic Movement Committee of the Protestant Churches in China (TSPM) (中国基督教三自爱国运动委员会) and China Christian Council (CCC) (中国基督教协会). The "Three-Self" principle requires Protestant churches in China to be free from foreign influence by being "self-administering, self-supporting, and self-propagating."

[58] For more on the Christian religious associations, see "The Three-Self Churches and 'Freedom' of Religion in China, 1980–1997," *Chinese Law and Government* 33, no. 6 (Nov/Dec 2000), which includes English translations of fifteen documents issued by the religious associations.

[59] The Public Security Bureau and the People's High Court of Jilin Province issued a notice "Notice to Strike Hard on Illegal Organizations" in May 2002 to such an effect. *See* http://www.china21.org/simpChinese/docs/0501_document_jilin.htm.

them illegal.[60] In the late 1990s, the rise of Falungong presented the bluntest challenge to the government and Party.[61] Falungong staged demonstrations outside government offices in Beijing in April 1999, and the government responded by rounding up local Falungong organizers.[62] In October 1999, the Standing Committee of the National People's Congress passed a "Legislative Resolution Banning Heretic Cults."[63] Since then, the government has focused on enforcement on all groups labeled as "evil cult" organizations (邪教组织), many of them *qigong* (气功) groups or underground religious groups. Many of those arrested are charged with "subverting the state," "using a cult organization to sabotage implementation of the law," or "endangering public order."[64]

Folk Religions and "Feudal Superstitions"

Since the founding of the PRC in 1949, the Party has sought to lessen the influence of a host of folk religious practices. Religious policy defines religion as having certain characteristics such as a written history, a scriptural canon, a set of doctrines, and a defined code of practice.[65] Authorities label practices falling outside this definition as "feudal superstitions" (封建迷信), referring to the pre-Communist "feudal" system of social organization. These practices include worship of ancestors, ritual worship of various local gods, or a combination of several of these indigenous practices, often mixed with Buddhism, Daoism, and community traditions. In most cases, publicity campaigns are used to convince individuals of the error of their ways, with varying degrees of success. In some cases, where the practices are deemed to be a threat to safety or social order, individuals such as fortune-tellers have been arrested and prosecuted under the Criminal Code. The exception, as mentioned earlier, is when national minorities practice these religions. However, the latest Beijing Religious Regulation (2002) dropped the clause of banned "superstition activities," and it seems to allow activities such as fortune telling or palmistry to operate openly under the category of cultural heritage. At the

---

[60] Included were the Shouters (呼喊派), Full-Scope Church (全范围教会), New Testament Church (新约教会) Eastern Lightning (东方闪电), Society of Disciples (门徒会), Spirit Church (灵灵教), and Guanyin Famen (观音法门). Later orders banned the Established King Church (被立王), Family of Love (爱的家庭), Dami Mission (达迷宣教会), and the Lord God Sect (主神教). See The Dui Hua Foundation, *Selection of Cases from the Criminal Law: Banned Protestant Groups*, February 2003.

[61] For a brief background on the social, economic, and political factors that influenced the rise of Falungong, see Ming Xia & Shiping Hua, "Guest Editors' Introduction," *Chinese Law and Government* 32, no. 5 (Sept/Oct 1999), 5–13.

[62] Neither the government nor Falungong considers Falungong a religion: the government regards it as an illegal cult; Falungong generally regards itself as a spiritual movement. *See* Shiping Hua & Ming Xia, "Guest Editors' Introduction," *Chinese Law and Government* 32, no. 5 (Nov/Dec 1999), 8–10.

[63]全国人民代表大会常务委员会关于取缔邪教组织, 防范和惩 治邪教活动的决定 (Decision of the Standing Committee of the National People's Congress on Banning Cult Organizations, Guarding Against and Punishing Cult Activities), *China Daily*, 30 Oct 1999.

[64] See Dui Hua Foundation, Selection of Cases from the Criminal Law. The Chinese terms are 颠覆国家政权, 利用邪教组织破坏法律实施, and 危害社会治安. See also "Criminal Verdict of the People's Court of Yunyang County, Chongqing City," translated in *Chinese Law and Government* 36, no. 3 (May/Jun 2003), 90–98.

[65] Chan Kim-Kwong and Alan Hunter, "Religion and Society in Mainland China in the 1990s," *Issues and Studies* 30 (Aug 1994), 53–54.

recent Religious Work Conference held in January 2004, the Government decided to set up a unit within SARA to deal with folk religions. It seems that the Chinese authorities are not only relaxing their enforcement efforts over folk religion and "feudal superstition" activities, but also trying to regulate these activities under the governmental superstition.

ADMINISTRATIVE DIVISIONS

China is comprised of 31 provincial-level entities: 22 provinces, 4 municipalities (Beijing, Shanghai, Tianjin, Chongq-ing), and 5 autonomous regions (Guangxi, Inner Mongolia/Nei Menggu, Ningxia, Xinjiang, Tibet/Xijang). Each of these entities is further subdivided into cities, municipal districts/prefecture districts, counties, townships, and villages. At each level, both the CPC and the government have parallel offices and divisions. Religious Affairs Bureaus have branches extending even to the village level, depending on the level of religious activities, with designated cadres at each level. Similarly, the UFWD has its own branches extending down to similar levels. Theoretically speaking, all "normal" religious activities are under the supervision of Party organs and government RABs and can claim the right of religious belief as enshrined in Party's policies and various SARA regulations. But each province runs its own local government and each municipality is endowed with a rather high degree of autonomy. In reality, then, these regulations and policies are subjected to a wide range of interpretations by local cadres, whose religious knowledge ranges from well versed to totally ignorant. These local government cadres interpret and implement the religious policies that affect the daily affairs of religious believers.

Due to problems in coordination across all levels in a country as large as China, the implementation of the Party's very same policy on freedom of religious belief can range from endorsement of religion to suppression. Local politics dictate the final outcome of religious policy. It may be possible to operate a religious group-operated orphanage in one county but not in the neighboring one. It may be possible to print religious literature in one province but not necessarily in the next one. A religious group may be legally registered in one province, but a group with the same teachings may be regarded as an "evil cult" by cadres in the neighboring province and thus subjected to criminal prosecution. Therefore, one needs to be extremely careful in interpreting the implementation of religious policies, as China is composed of thousands of local governments with cadres of varying levels of administrative skill and technical knowledge of religion. Usually, the higher the administration level, the closer the administration of religious affairs would conform to the national government's stated religious policy; the lower the administrative level, the more latitude that local administrator would decide on religious administration based on local sociopolitical dynamics.

SECTION TWO:
CHINA'S RELIGIOUS POLICY: THEORY AND IMPLEMENTATION

Religious Policy before Deng Xiaoping

Throughout history, Chinese governments have played a very active role in supervising, regulating, and sometimes suppressing religion.[66] Traditional Chinese religions centered on Daoism and folk religions (including ancestor worship). Buddhism and Islam were introduced into China many centuries ago.[67] While Christian missionaries have been in China for several hundred years, they have long been politically associated with Western imperialism and colonialism. Beginning with the Opium Wars in the 1840s and through World War I, Western nations carved out spheres of influence in China. The Japanese invasions and atrocities before and during World War II culminated China's "century of humiliation" at the hands of foreigners.

The PRC was established in 1949 and CPC doctrine, following Marxist-Leninist Thought, promoted atheism. But Mao realized that religion was not a problem that would instantly disappear. Instead, he attempted to co-opt religion using the United Front Theory, creating patriotic religious associations to ensure that religious influence stayed within government-set parameters. Religious policy in the early years of the PRC featured a combination of a moderate approach to those who would be co-opted and a militant approach to those who would not.[68] The excesses of the Cultural Revolution (1966–1976) brought the most violent hostility toward religion, with Red Guards destroying churches, mosques, and temples with equal harshness in an attempt to eradicate the traditional culture and heritage embodied in the "Four Olds."[69]

After 1978, when Deng Xiaoping consolidated power, the state treated religion more liberally but still within the confines of state supervision. For the post-Mao era, religious policy can be divided into three main periods: first, the period from 1982, when China's current constitution and Document No. 19 were written, until the Tiananmen Square incident in 1989; second, the period from 1989, with the Tiananmen Square incident in China and the fall of communism elsewhere, until the end of the century, when Falungong openly challenged the government; and third, from 2000 to the present, when the Party adopted Jiang's "Three Represents" Theory, began to institute the rule of law, joined the WTO, and implemented other modernizations in China, while banning

---

[66] For a concise history, see R. Lanier Britsch, "The Current Legal Status of Christianity in China," *BYU Law Review* 1995, 347–48 (1995); Chan Kim-Kwong, "A Chinese Perspective on the Interpretation of the Chinese Government's Religious Policy," in *All Under Heaven: Chinese Tradition and Christian Life in the People's Republic of China* (Alan Hunter and Don Rimmington, eds. 1992), 38.
[67] *See* Chan Kim-Kwong and Alan Hunter, "Religion and Society in Mainland China in the 1990s," *Issues and Studies* 30 (Aug 1994), 52–68.
[68] *See* Beatrice Leung, "Religious Freedom and the Constitution in the People's Republic of China: Interpretation and Implementation," *DISKUS* 3:1 (1995), 1–18.
[69] The "Four Olds" were old ideas, old culture, old customs, and old habits.

"cult" organizations. The emphasis is on the third period as the current policy may have more practical applications for contemporary scholars.[70]

1982–1989

After Deng Xiaoping began to consolidate power, China began to revamp the legal structures that had collapsed during the Cultural Revolution. In March 1982, the CPC Central Committee issued "Document No. 19: The Basic Policy and Standpoint Our Country Should Have on the Religious Question During This Period of Socialism." This long-term approach toward religion asserted that coercive means should not be used to extinguish religion (retreating from the excesses of the Cultural Revolution). Rather, religion should exist within state-controlled parameters. The document also acknowledged "leftist" errors ("左" 的错误) in dealing with religion in the past. It stressed the five "natures"[71] of religion and the necessity of using patriotic religious associations coordinated by the United Front Work Department. State-supervised religion would be tolerated within limits, but activities outside state-defined limits would be repressed. This important document forms the foundation of all post-Mao religious policy.[72]

In December 1982, China's fourth constitution was ratified. Article 36 asserts that the State protects "normal religious activities." However, the Article continues, "[n]o one may make use of religion to engage in activities that disrupt public order, impair the health of citizens or interfere with the educational system of the state. Religious bodies and religious affairs are not subject to any foreign domination."[73] The 1982 constitution thus theoretically provided the basis for freedom of religious belief—within the parameters of government control.[74]

Officially, the religious policy has three main themes: first, the state respects both the freedom to believe in religion and the freedom not to belief in religion; second, the state neither promotes nor suppresses any particular religion; and third, it emphasizes the principle of the self-administration and autonomy of religious affairs in China. This policy allows the five recognized religions to operate under the government-recognized patriotic religious associations, which follow the political objectives of the State. Further,

---

[70] For a more complete history, see http://www.china.org.cn/e-white/Freedom/index.htm.

[71] The five natures are long-term nature (长期性), mass nature (群众性), ethnic nature (民族性), international nature (国际性), and complex nature (复杂性).

[72] Chan Kim-Kwong and Alan Hunter, "New Light on Religious Policy in the PRC," *Issues and Studies* 31 (Feb 1995), 24. See also Philip L. Wickeri, *Seeking the Common Ground: Protestant Christianity, the Three-Self Movement, and China's United Front* (1988), 88.

[73] Constitution of the People's Republic of China (1982), Article 36. The PRC's three previous constitutions also included explicit provisions for freedom of religious belief: 1954 (Article 99), 1975 (Article 28), and 1978 (Article 46).

[74] Other constitutional provisions that could possibly infringe upon unlimited freedom of religious belief include Article 15 (prohibiting disturbance of the socioeconomic order), Article 28 (punishing activities that endanger public order or state security), Article 25 (promoting family planning), Article 51 (stipulating that rights and freedoms cannot infringe upon the interests of the state or society), and Article 54 (prohibiting acts "detrimental to the security, honor, and interests of the motherland"). Constitution of the People's Republic of China (1982).

no foreign body can have any claim over religion in China; such a policy places strains on religious groups that have international ties, such as the Catholic Church. Compared to the Cultural Revolution era, the policy of the 1980s was quite conciliatory and pragmatic, and many religious groups, especially Christian, sprung up from this liberalization.

1989–2000

By the late 1980s, the CPC became increasingly concerned by the rising tide of various religious groups, especially those with foreign ties. Religion could become an independent source of power outside the Party's organizational monopoly, challenge the Party at the local level as a basic social network, be used by ethnic groups to clamor for further autonomy, and threaten communist ideology.[75] Even more worrisome, Party leaders were concerned about the role religion could play in fomenting social unrest, particularly the influence foreigners had on domestic religions with possibly political motives, such as advocacy of democracy. Further, the Berlin Wall fell in the same year as the Tiananmen Square incident (1989), and communism in Eastern Europe fell soon after. China sent social scientists to the countries of Eastern Europe and the former Soviet Union to study the factors that contributed to the downfall of communism. The scholars concluded that the West had intentionally sabotaged communism through many factors, gradually eroding the pillars of socialism through a process of "peaceful evolution" (和平演变) from communism to capitalist democracies. These factors include economic pressures, the Voice of America, religious groups, and international organizations. The scholars particularly found that religious groups (e.g., the Catholic Church in Poland and Czechoslovakia, the Reform Church in Hungary, the Lutheran Church in Germany) were influential in contributing to the collapse of socialism, since Western powers had supported these religious groups to instigate democratic movements against communism. The Chinese scholars regarded officials in the eastern bloc as too ignorant of powerful Western influences, including religion.

There are scholarly disagreements as to the validity of this peaceful evolution theory, but it has at least some measure of truth, and Chinese leaders were concerned that the same thing might occur in China. The documents of this period—both public and internal—reflect this desire to prevent peaceful evolution: "Document No. 3: Stepping up Control over the Catholic Church to Meet the New Situation"; "Hebei Province: Provisions to Safeguard the Normal Religious Activities of the Catholic Church"; "Document No. 6: Some Problems Concerning Further Improving Work on Religion;" and "Regulations on the Supervision of Religious Activities of Foreigners in China."[76] China likely saw the efforts of international organizations (such as the UN Human Rights Committee) and NGOs (such as Human Rights Watch, The Soros Fund, The Heritage Foundation) around the world that promote human rights and religious freedom as evidence of the West's intent to undermine socialism through "peaceful evolution."

President Jiang Zemin's address to the National United Front Work Conference in November 1993 marked a subtle shift in religious policy. Called the "Three Phrases,"

---

[75] Chan Kim-Kwong and Alan Hunter, "New Light on Religious Policy in the PRC," *Issues and Studies* 31 (Feb 1995), 22.

[76] See *infra* Section Three for more details on these documents.

Jiang emphasized: (1) implement the Party's religious policy thoroughly and correctly; (2) strengthen control of religious affairs according to the law; and (3) positively guide religion to be compatible with socialist society.[77]

In January 1994, the State Council promulgated two decrees based on President Jiang's "Three Phrases": Decree 144: "Regulations on the Management of Religious Activities of Foreigners in China," and Decree 145: "Regulations on the Management of Places of Religious Activities." Taken together, these regulations reflect an effort to clarify and delineate legal and illegal religious activity, particularly with regard to acceptable religious contacts with foreigners. These regulations do not, however, reflect a significant change in government policy, nor do the regulations eliminate all interpretive uncertainties.[78]

In 1995, the Shanghai RAB drafted the first clearly written regional religious regulation,[79] incorporating responsibility, accountability, fines, and so forth as part of an effort to upgrade the rule of law and popularize knowledge of law and legal systems (普法). After its issuance, many provincial and municipal RAB cadres traveled to Shanghai to learn about the drafting process; many returned to their locales and used the Shanghai model. These post-1995 regulations were certainly far from perfect, omitting, among other things, responsibility for enforcement and the final source of fines. This was also part of a government effort to devolve power to the provinces, allowing them to craft regulations with a local "flavor." Thus, regional religious regulations differ in some subtle aspects from Tibet to Guangdong.[80]

Religious regulations before 1994/1995 were more restrictive toward religion and disparately enforced. By the mid- to late-1990s, Jiang Zemin and the "third generation" of Chinese leaders recognized the need for continued modernizations and the importance of the rule of law, particularly in securing entry into the World Trade Organization (WTO). Religious policy began to reflect this as one can notice the appearance of various regional religious regulations since 1995 with higher degree of clarity than those previously issued. Further, Documents No. 19 and No. 6 reflected internal policy documents rather than official statements of law. Thus there was a need to translate and publicize these policies as China attempted to implement the rule of law.

---

[77] The phrases in Chinese are 正确地贯彻执行党的宗教政策, 依法加强对宗教事务的管理, and 积极引导宗教与社会主义社会相适应.

[78] Chan Kim-Kwong and Alan Hunter, "New Light on Religious Policy in the PRC," *Issues and Studies* 31 (Feb 1995), 26–27.

[79] An English translation of the Shanghai regulation is available. See Shanghai Municipality People's Congress, "Shanghai Religious Affairs Bureau Rules," 30 Nov 1995, translation by *Tripod*, vol. XVI, No. 92, at http://www.hrw.org/reports/1997/china1. A different translation is available at *Chinese Law and Government* 33, no. 3 (May/Jun 2000), 12–16. *See infra* Section Three for more details.

[80] For example, the 1995 Shanghai regulation has clear provisions banning "feudal superstition activities" such as palmistry, geomancy, or fortune-telling, whereas the 2002 Beijing regulation has no such provisions. Such difference reflects not only the regional differences in understanding of religion, but more importantly, the changes in understanding regarding religious activities since the mid-1990s. Mr. Zhao Kanwei, a former researcher at SARA, has commented that society in general seemed to adopt a more liberal view on religion than before. Remarks at the International Conference on Chinese Culture and Development, held in Shanghai, 18 September 2003.

2000–present

China began to subtly refine its religious policy as it sought entry into the World Trade Organization. WTO accession would usher in a whole new range of social challenges for the Chinese government—from labor unrest of unemployed workers to the tensions caused by economic polarization. Accession to the WTO could also have a large impact on religious regulations and may even call their legitimacy into question. The Chinese government faces unprecedented challenges to lead China back into the international community as a significant power and to maintain the Party's absolute leadership over China. In the past few years, the Chinese government has completed a series of post-WTO accession assessments and formulated policies on the above-mentioned political objectives. With the exception of Falungong and other "cults," religion had long been relegated to a relatively minor social issue until December 2001, when President Jiang Zemin called a Religious Work Conference attended by the full Politburo, as well as the top leaders from all branches of the government, Party and military.[81] This Conference signaled a refinement of religious policy to face the predicted religious growth in the context of social adjustment following WTO. There have been debates within the Party as to what the religious policy should be when China enters the WTO: should the Chinese government let go of its control over religion, just as the government has done in economic matters, merging China into the globalized world order? Or should the government suppress the growth of religion?[82]

Just prior to the Religious Work Conference, Jiang put forward a new theory called the "Three Represents" as the CPC's newest guiding principle.[83] The theory justified the CPC as the only governing party for the good of China. In 2002, the Sixteenth Party Congress formally adopted this "Three Represents" Theory as the Party's doctrine, along with a charge for the whole nation to integrate such doctrine into practice. In spring 2003, SARA has generated a series of study materials putting the new religious policy in the context of the Party's new thinking on the "Three Represents."[84] Ye Xiaowen, the director-general of SARA, wrote several influential commentaries on the role of religion interpreting the adjusted policy in the context of the "Three Represents" Theory.[85] The current policy as outlined by Jiang and explicated by Ye emphasizes three

---

[81] The full report of this Conference as well as the speech made by Jiang is published in *Renmin Ribao* (People's Daily), 13 December 2002. The subsequent articles were published in the Party's internal bulletin *Tongxin* (Communication), January 2002, 1–20.

[82] After all, according to Party orthodoxy, religion is supposed to be an unscientific worldview hindering societal progress needing eradication.

[83] Jiang's "Three Represents" Theory asserts that the Communist Party represents the advanced productive forces, advanced culture, and the interests of the masses. For more details, see http://www.china.org.cn/english/features/48209.htm.

[84] One of the most important articles is by SARA Director-General Ye Xiaowen: 对社会主义社会宗教问题的重新认识深刻思考 (A Deep Reflection and a New Understanding of Religious Issues in Socialist Society), 理论动态(*Theoretical Dynamics*), 10 Jan 2003, 1–12. This journal is a classified publication by the Party's Academy for internal circulation among senior cadres. The subsequent study materials from SARA are all written within the parameters established in the Introduction of this article.

[85]Ye Xiaowen, 社会主义的宗教论 (Socialism's View of Religion), *China Religion*, May 2003, page 6; Ye Xiaowen, 为什么要钻研 «社会主义的宗教论 (Why We Must Careful Study 'Socialism's View of Religion), *China Religion*, May 2003, page 12.

of the five natures of religion: long-term nature, mass nature, and complex nature. Ye's article rephrases the new religious policy in Chinese Communist rhetoric. First, since religion has a long-term nature, it will exist for a long period of time; thus, the CPC should activity guide religion to adapt itself to socialist society.[86] Second, since the critical issue for religion is its mass nature,[87] the CPC should vigorously implement the Party's policy on religious belief. Third, since religion is complex and unique, the CPC should emphasize the legislative nature of religious policy, stressing the independent nature of religion in China, and nonsanctioned religions should be suppressed by legal and administrative means. An interpretation and explication of communist terminology is appropriate for each of these three policies.

First, the government openly acknowledges that religion has existed and will continue to exist as part of human civilization, and that government's role is to "actively guide religion to adapt itself to socialist society." The policy is an admission that communism may not hold a monopoly on absolute truth as asserted before by the Party, especially on understanding of religion.[88] Further, religion is a cultural force that cannot be eliminated by administrative means. The Party here takes a pragmatic stance on religion not dissimilar similar to the Party's position on economic matters by adopting a market economy and baptizing it as "socialism with Chinese characteristics." The government will not encourage the development of religion—but will not suppress all religion by force. Rather, the Party would continue to actively promote the truth—scientific materialism and atheism—to the masses. On this point, this new policy stressed a categorical difference between Party members and religious believers: no religious believer can be a Party member and vice versa.

The policy repeatedly emphasizes the slogan that "religion and socialist society must mutually adapt."[89] This means that religion must adapt itself to Chinese socialist society, and Chinese socialist society must also adjust to the presence of religion. In the Chinese reality, though, the government defines what adaptation is required by what religion, even to the extent that a religion must change or modify its teachings and practices to suit the Party's political objectives.[90]

The government also recognizes that religions must assist in cushioning the societal transformations brought on by China's WTO accession while preventing unwanted foreign influences from infiltrating. The policy also recognizes that WTO

[86] *See* Luo Shuze, "Some Hot Issues in Our Work on Religion," *Qiushi*, no. 5 (1996), translated in *Chinese Law and Government* 33, no. 2 (Mar/Apr 2000), 103–04.

[87] China has more than 200 million religious adherents. U.S. State Department, International Religious Freedom Report 2003: China, at http://www.state.gov/g/drl/rls/irf/2004/35396.htm.

[88] This policy did not touch upon the thorny issue of the nature of religion because such discussion would challenge the fundamental interpretation of religion. That is, if religion is a distorted worldview, as the Party has insisted in the past, and religion would disappear with social progress, how does the existence of religion in a developed society relate to Communist teachings on religion?

[89] The phrase in Chinese is 宗教与社会主义社会相适应.

[90] In compliance with the government's supervision over religious matters, some religious associations in China began to change their individual constitutions to reflect this political reality. For example, the China Christian Council amended its constitution in May 2002 to include the wording: "This Council accepts the legal administrative authority of the State Administration of Religious Affairs . . . ." Chapter One, Article Five of the revised CCC Constitution. One of the general guidelines to religious groups is to help the country with economic development, such as to introduce foreign investors to China and to contribute to charitable projects such as poverty alleviation efforts.

accession may trigger a new wave of foreign religious influences. The government will make every effort to resist such influence—in contrast to the government's policies in other sectors such as the economy and commerce, where there is effort to take in foreign elements to enable a smooth integration into the global market. China's religious associations have adopted this concept into their policies in relating to foreign counterparts.[91] Director-General Ye has stressed that the Chinese Church must step up its anti-infiltration (反渗透) efforts to block hostile foreign groups from establishing footholds in China.[92] Simultaneously, the Church must cultivate positive relationships with friendly foreign religious bodies to promote the policies and achievements of China.

Second, because religious believers are numerous, the Party should implement religious policy carefully to contain religious activities in a defined area of operation. The policy is thus freedom of religious belief, not freedom of religious expression. Religion is tolerated so long as it posts no threat to the ruling regime and no challenge to the present social institutions such as education and marriage. This policy is meant to keep religion out of the sociopolitical domain.

Third, the CPC recognizes that religion is a complex phenomenon, so religious affairs must be carefully managed in accordance with the law: both recognized religions and nonsanctioned religions will be dealt with according to objective criteria. The Party recognizes the complex relations between religious bodies in China and their overseas counterparts. The government will continue to monitor Chinese religions bodies to ensure that they maintain their independence and block infiltration efforts by foreign mission groups.[93]

The Party/government uses legislative means to establish the boundaries for "normal" religions. "Normal" religions within these boundaries must register with the patriotic religious associations and SARA to claim religious protection. Groups falling outside these boundaries may be considered "cult organizations" and prosecuted by law.[94] Some of these indigenous groups are magnets for dissatisfied workers, the unemployed or poverty-stricken peasants who may cling to exotic yet hopeful teachings. The government recognizes that these new groups could be potentially destabilizing, both as challenges to the state's organizational monopoly and though eschatological teachings that confront the regime's legitimacy. The government regulates these groups on the basis of national security rather than religion.[95]

Foreigners have introduced other internationally established and recognized religious groups. Because they are not part of the five recognized religious associations,

---

[91] The new president of the China Christian Council (CCC), Reverend Cao Shengjie, has made strong remarks on "foreign infiltration" in the CCC/TSPM Working Report concerning the direction of the CCC in future relations with foreign religious groups. See "Working Report of the Executive Committee of TSMP/CCC" May 2002, Beijing; *see also Tianfeng* no. 7 (July 2002), 4–10.

[92] Ye Xiaowen, "Opening Speech at the Seventh Chinese Protestant Representative Conference," May 22, 2002, in *Religion in China*, no. 4, 2002, 11–13.

[93] *See* Luo Shuze, "Some Hot Issues in Our Work on Religion," *Qiushi*, no. 5 (1996), as translated in *Chinese Law and Government* 33, no. 2 (Mar/Apr 2000), 101–02.

[94] Article 300 of the Chinese Criminal Code.

[95] See *Notification on Certain Questions Regarding the Identification and Elimination of Evil Cults*, National Public Security Bureau (institutional secret), 30 April 2000, 1–22, available at http://www.china21.org.

these groups have an uncertain legal status, both for expatriate and local believers.[96] Although they have no official registration, they are often allowed to operate with knowledge and tacit approval of local PSB and RAB authorities. The government recognizes the legal and political consequences of recognizing these groups, thereby possibly opening a Pandora's box that may stress the current policy on religion beyond its limit—when any religious group could claim the benefits of official recognition.

On November 30, 2004, Premiere Wen Jiabao approved new "Religious Affairs Regulations," effective nationwide on March 1, 2005.[97] These regulations serve as national guidelines for religious administration. The regulations continue the general scheme of state supervision and administration. The new national regulations generally codify and standardize provisions found in provincial regulations and clarify the scope of government oversight and provide some avenues of appeals for administrative decisions, though the vagueness of these rights and the uncertainty of effective legal recourse leaves much to be desired. For groups outside the established registration scheme, however, the regulations provide no additional protections. In fact, unregistered religions may be worse off, as the regulations give less room for maneuvering in gray areas in the prior ambiguous rules.

The government is also expanding and upgrading the Religious Affairs Bureau in anticipation of the growth of religion in China. RAB cadres across the nation have studied religious policy as it relates to the "Three Represents" Theory.[98] High-ranking Politburo officials have given their blessing to the continuation of the current religious policy.[99]

---

[96] Examples of such groups are Ba'hai, Judaism, and The Church of Jesus Christ of Latter-day Saints (the LDS Church).

[97] After six years of drafting, these regulations were approved by the Executive Meeting of the State Council in July 2004 and made public in mid-December 2004. *See* Xinhua News Agency, "Religious Affairs Provisions to Take Effect Next March," December 19, 2004, at http://www.china.org.cn/english/2004/Dec/115343.htm. For the complete text (Chinese and English translation) of these regulations, see the Appendix of this volume.

[98] One of the most important source of material on religious policy vis-à-vis the "Three Represents" Theory is the 561-page study volume published by SARA: 宗教工作的理论与实践: 2003 年全国宗教工作理论务虚会论文集 (Theory and Practice of Religious Work: Collection of Papers from the 2003 National Conference on Religious Work Theory).

[99] The chairman of the National Committee of the powerful Chinese People's Political Consultative Conference (CPPCC) has affirmed the government's support of the "Three Represents" principle in religious policy. *See* Jia Qinglin's speech at the 2004 National Religious Work Conference, in "Jia Qinglin Emphasizes 'Three Represents' in Leading Religious Work," *Renmin Ribao*, 7 January 2004, 1.

Section Three: The Sources

Regulations are the major primary source documents for religious administration in China. Nearly all national level regulations and most regional regulations are published; many are available on the Internet. Nearly every jurisdiction that has a Religious Affairs Bureau also has regulations that govern the management of religious affairs. As the size of geographical jurisdiction becomes smaller, so does the likelihood of widespread publication, if at all. Many local level regulations are published only in small numbers; some are simply fixed to the door of the local Religious Affairs Bureau or town hall.

No single source contains all of the regulations. A book published in 2000, 全国宗教行政法规规章汇编 (*Compilation of National Administrative Rules and Regulations on Religion*), lists some fifty national and provincial regulations related to religion. The United Front Web site's section on religious laws[100] lists about fifty-five regulations related to religion (there is a large overlap with the aforementioned book). The newly promulgated national Religious Affairs Regulations can found in the Appendix of this volume. The Religion and Law Research Consortium Web site[101] sponsored by an association of U.S. and Western European church-state scholars, hosts a searchable database of constitution, laws, and regulations from around the world that affect religion. The Web site is in the ongoing process of posting nearly 200 regulations and other religion-related documents from China and other countries. Other regulations can be found by visiting the respective Web sites of a targeted jurisdiction. Several years ago, the Chinese government made a push for provincial and local governments to host Web sites, and now most governments at the city/county level and above have acceptable Web sites. There does not seem to be any (discernable) systematized approach to government Web addresses or Web page formatting, so the user is largely relegated to searching jurisdiction by jurisdiction or through search engines.

This Handbook will list all the published religious regulations through the year 2004 issued at the national and regional levels under **National Regulations, Related Regulations and Guidelines,** and **Regional Regulations**. Although different cities and counties may have their own regulations (mostly local versions of the corresponding provincial regulation), it would be impractical to list them all, for they may run into thousands. Other than religious regulations, many other laws and regulations have also touch on religious matters. For example, the Custom Law has regulations concerning the importation of religious literature into China, and the Marriage Law has a clause that prohibits discrimination against religious faith. Major laws issued at the national level will be included as part of the National Regulations section.

The section on **Government and Party Documents, Notices and Decisions** includes those Party documents and decisions that may have a stronger bearing on religious administration than regulations. In some situations, cadres follow these notices

---

[100] 宗教政策与法规 (Religious Policy and Regulations), at http://www.zytzb.org.cn/zytzbwz/flfg.

[101] Religion and Law Research Consortium, at http://www.religlaw.org.

and decisions in lieu of following the regulations. When a regulation is passed, it is also interpreted through the principles laid down by these documents. Apart from these documents, Party and government leaders often issue **Commentary and Policy Directives**, often in the form of speeches by national leaders. The principles in these speeches often become de facto rules. There is a whole range of **Party and Government Publications** on religious affairs. These materials often become the study materials for the cadres on religious affairs, and these publications provide a glimpse of how government officials comprehend and interpret these regulations and policies. Some of these publications are issues for internal (classified) reference and some are for public consumption; those classified publications listed here are available to bona fide scholars at the Universities Service Center of the Chinese University of Hong Kong. The public security apparatus also issues **Public Security-Related Documents, Manuals, and Publications**, mainly targeting "cult organizations" and other unregistered religious groups. These regulations and directives are usually highly classified materials not intended for public knowledge. However, some of these documents have already made way to the academic circles and are available on the Internet. Finally, **Secondary Sources** include books and journal articles in Chinese and English that help a researcher better understand the whole situation of religious policy and religious liberty in China. Most of the publications listed at this section are not published in China. Finally, there is a section on **Internet Sources** that lists sites relevant to religious freedom in China. All Web sites have been verified as of December 21, 2004.

A note on the classified materials: The Chinese government issues classified directives and documents that are not disclosed to the public. Often the existence of these documents is not supposed to be known to unauthorized persons. Any unauthorized possession, disclosure, or sharing of these materials is a crime that may be prosecuted under Article 282 of China's Criminal Code.[102] However, many of these "classified" documents have been circulated outside of China and are readily available on the Internet or in printed format. This Handbook will list those documents that are publicly available outside of China. However, the authenticity and accuracy of these materials depend on the judgment of individual scholars. This Handbook merely lists those allegedly classified documents while making no endorsement regarding their authenticity.

A note on translation: Chinese titles of the sources have been translated. Some of the more important documents have been translated by several different authors and thus have slightly different titles.

[102] *See* People's Republic of China, *Protection of State Secrets Act*, passed by the National People's Congress of People's Republic of China on 5 September 1998, effective 1 May 1999.

Regulations

National Regulations

Regulations are listed in reverse chronological order. The most important regulations are in **bold.**

宗教事務條例 (Religious Affairs Provisions), issued as Decree 426 of the State Council on November 30, 2004, and effective nationwide on March 1, 2005. These regulations are the first to list out the duties and responsibilities of SARA/RAB on religious administration, as well as the rights and obligations of registered religious organizations. It is to serve as the national standard for all religious affairs administration. The complete Chinese text and English can be found in the Appendix. Decree 145, listed below, will automatically be nullified when these regulations come into effect.

境内外国人宗教活动管理规定实施细则 (Specific Rules for Implementing the Regulations on the Management of Religious Activities of Foreigners in China), 26 Sep 2000
This SARA regulation expanded the list of impermissible activities for aliens to include the following: appointing religious personnel among Chinese citizens, developing religious following among Chinese citizens, preaching/expounding scripture at sites of religious activities without permission, and reading/expounding scripture outside lawfully registered sites. The rules were published in the People's Daily Overseas Edition, 27 Sep 2000, page 1. An English translation was published in China Daily, 27 Sep 2000, page 1. (Note that the document was published in English and in Chinese in an overseas edition, but not in the mainstream media on the mainland.)

宗教活动场所年度检查办法 (Procedures for the Annual Inspection of Venues of Religious Activity), 29 Jul 1996
This regulation requires annual inspections for all venues of religious activity. The inspection checks, among other things, that the organization is not "conducting religious or foreign-related activity which is illegal or against the rules." An English translation by UCA News is available in Human Rights Watch, China: State Control of Religion (1997) Appendix IX; also at http://www.hrw.org/reports/1997/china1.

中华人民共和国境内外国人宗教活动管理规定 (Decree 144 of State Council: Regulations on the Management of Religious Activities of Foreigners in China), 31 Jan 1994
This decree allows foreigners to participate in religious activities in China, but prohibits them from establishing religious organizations, liaison offices, and venues for religious activities, or running religious schools and institutions within China, recruiting believers,

appointing clergy, or undertaking evangelic activities. It is another example of anti-infiltration efforts taken by the government to prevent foreign influences and peaceful evolution. The decree was published in *Renmin Ribao* [People's Daily] on 8 Feb 1994, page 3; it can also be found in 新时期宗教工作文献选编 (Collection of Literature on Religious Work in the New Era) (see below for book details). An English translation by the Amity News Service (an outlet of the China Christian Council) can be found at http://www.amityfoundation.org/ANS/Religious%20Laws/reg1.htm.

宗教活动场所管理条例 (Decree 145 of State Council: Regulations on the Management of Places of Religious Activities), 31 Jan 1994
This decree requires SARA approval for the establishment of venues of religious activity; registration requires having a suitable building, regular meetings and attendance, proper organization, professional leadership, governing rules, regular income, and payment of a registration fee. Many local regulations and memos have interpreted Decree 145 to mean all sites not approved by the government are treated as illegal. The decree was published in 人民日报[People's Daily] on 8 Feb 1994, page 3; in can also be found in 新时期宗教工作文献选编 (Collection of Literature on Religious Work in the New Era) (see below for book details). An English translation by the Amity News Service (an outlet of the China Christian Council) can be found at
http://www.amityfoundation.org/ANS/Religious%20Laws/reg2.htm.
According to additional regulations promulgated by SARA on 13 Apr 1994, 宗教活动场所登记办法, registration also requires the blessing of local government. A translation of the supplement can be found at
http://www.amityfoundation.org/ANS/Religious%20Laws/reg3.htm.

Related Regulations and Guidelines

关于党员,党员干部对宗教信仰问题的原则和态度 (Regarding Party Members' and Party Cadres' Basic Principles and Attitudes Toward Religious Belief), 12 Aug 2004 (CPC Central Committee)

关于加强对宗教事务工作领导的若于意见的通知 (Notification Regarding Certain Opinions on Strengthening the Leadership over Religious Affairs Work), 17 Aug 2004 (State Council and Central Government Office)

关于大专院校宗教团体和宗教活动的若于意见 (Certain Opinions Regarding Religious Organizations and Religious Activities in Universities, Colleges, and Institutes), 21 Aug 2004 (State Council and Ministry of Education)

These three abovementioned documents are referenced in the September 2004 issue of the Hong Kong magazine «争鸣» (Zeng Ming), pages 20–22. These alleged regulations suggest a tightening of religious administration, including absolutely forbidding CPC cadres to embrace religious belief. The full text of these alleged documents is not available at this time.

关于取缔邪教组织, 防范和惩治邪教活动的决定 (Resolution Concerning the Banning of Cult Organizations, Prevention Measures Against Them, and Punishment for Cult Activities), 30 Oct 1999
Passed by the Standing Committee of the National People's Congress, this short resolution banned "cults" operating "under the guise of religion, qigong or other illicit forms." The resolution differentiates between organizers and participants: the former is severely dealt with, the latter subject to re-education. This resolution appeared in *Renmin Ribao*, 31 Oct 1999 (http://www.people.com.cn/GB/channel1/10/20000706/132388.html.) An English translation was published in *China Daily* on 30 Oct 1999, http://www.amityfoundation.org/ANS/Religious%20Laws/reg4.htm.

最高人民法院,最高人民检察院 «关于办理组织和利用邪教组织犯罪案件具体应用法律若干问题的解释» (Supreme People's Court and Supreme People's Procuratorate: "Judicial Explanation on Crimes by Cults"), 4 Jun 2001
This short document is a judicial explanation of how Article 300 is to be administered. At http://www.people.com.cn/GB/shizheng/16/20010611/486116.html. An English translation is available at "Judicial Explanations on Crimes by Cults," *Chinese Law and Government* 36, no. 3 (May–June 2003): 87–89.

宗教院校聘用外籍专业人员办法 (Procedures for Religious Colleges and Institutions to Hire Foreign Specialists), 19 Nov 1998 http://www.zytzb.org.cn/zytzbwz/flfg/zj4ae.htm.

社会团体登记管理条例 (Regulations on the Management of Social Organization Registration), 25 Sep 1998 http://www.bast.cn.net/kjfg/gjkjfg/69.htm

关于在农村基层组织建设中认真妥善地处理好宗教活动问题的通知 (On Properly Dealing with Religious Activity Issues in Countryside Grass-Roots Units), 13 Jan 1998 http://www.ctnews.com.cn/webpub/template/aTpldef.asp?ID=3440&Cn=%D7%DA%BD%CC%B9%E6%B7%B6.

加强对含有宗教内容广告管理(Strengthening the Management of Religious Content Included in Advertising), 30 Apr 1997.
http://www.on118.com/LawDB/LawDetail.asp?ID=11294.

制止乱建庙宇和露天佛像的意见 (Ideas on Stopping the Random Construction of Buddhist Temples and Open-Air Buddha Statues), 13 Dec 1996

社会团体年度检查暂行办法 (Temporary Procedures for the Annual Inspection of Social Associations), 14 May 1996
In 宗教工作普法读本 (Religious Work Popular Law Reader) (see below for book details).

关于自费朝觐若干规定的通知 (Notice on Certain Stipulations on Paying One's Own Pilgrimage Expenses), 28 Jan 1995 http://www.qdtravel.com/inter/law/law34.shtm.

最高人民法院对国务院宗教事务局一司关于僧人遗产处理意见的复函 (Supreme People's Court Reply Letter to State Council: Opinion on Dealing with Buddhist Priests' Inheritance), 13 Oct 1994
http://law.chinalawinfo.com/newlaw2002/SLC/SLC.asp?Db=chl&Gid=15435.

中华人民共和国澳门特别行政区基本法 (节录) (Selections from PRC Macau SAR Basic Law), 31 Mar 1993
See Articles 25, 34, 128, 133, 134. In 新时期民族宗教工作宣传手册 (Propaganda Handbook on Nationality and Religious Work) (see below for book details).

关于城市建设中拆迁教堂、寺庙等房屋问题处理意见的通知 (Notice on Ideas and Issues on Dealing with Relocating Chapels, Temples, and Houses Amid Urban Construction), 20 Jan 1993.
http://law.chinalawinfo.com/newlaw2002/SLC/SLC.asp?Db=chl&Gid=15497.

宗教社会团体登记管理实施办法 (Procedures for Implementing the Management of Religious Organizations Registration), 6 May 1991.
In 新时期宗教工作文献选编 (Collection of Literature on Religious Work in the New Era) (see below for book details); The regulation is also online at
http://www.miaoyin.net/zhengcefagui/zongjiaoshehuituantidengjiguanlishixingbanfa.htm.

«中华人民共和国香港特别行政区基本法» 中有关宗教信仰自由的条款 (Provisions Relating to the Freedom of Religious Belief in the "PRC Hong Kong SAR Basic Law"), 4 Apr 1990
Relevant provisions in the Hong Kong Basic Law include Article 23 (requiring enactment of laws to prohibit foreign political organizations), Article 32 (protecting freedom of religious belief), Article 137 (protecting schools run by religious organizations), Article 141 (protecting religious organizations' rights to own property, run schools, maintain overseas ties, etc.), Article 148 (asserting that relationship between mainland and HK organizations must be based on the principles of non-subordination, non-interference and mutual respect), and Article 149 (protecting right of religious organizations to maintain ties with overseas counterparts). [See also Article 15 of the Hong Kong Bill of Rights Ordinance, which incorporates Article 18 of the ICCPR] These provisions can be found in 新时期民族宗教工作宣传手册 (Propaganda Handbook on Nationality and Religious Work) and online in many places, such as
http://www.hku.hk/law/conlawhk/sourcebook/ordinances.htm.

«人民检察院直接受理的侵犯公民民主权利,人身权利和渎职案件立案标准的规定» 第八条 (Article 8 of "Standard Filing Provisions for the People's Procuratorate to Directly Hear a Case of Violating a Citizen's Democratic Rights, Bodily Rights, and Malfeasance") 3 Nov 1989
Lays out exactly what constitutes violating a citizens rights, including forcing a person to believe or not believe in religion, or forcing a member of a minority group to change their customs. In 新时期宗教工作文献选编 (Collection of Literature on Religious Work in the New Era) (see below for book details)

制止丧葬中的封建迷信活动 (Stopping Feudal Superstitions During Funeral Ceremonies), 29 May 1989. http://www.on118.com/LawDB/LawDetail.asp?ID=4592.

全国人民代表大会外事委员会就欧洲议会通过所谓«关于西藏人权»决议的声明 (Statement of the National People's Congress External Affairs Committee About the European Parliament's Passage of the So-Called "Human Rights in Tibet" Resolution), 18 Mar 1989
In 新时期宗教工作文献选编 (Collection of Literature on Religious Work in the New Era) (see below for book details)

国务院关于第十世班禅大师治丧和转世问题的决定 (State Council Resolution on the Issues of Funeral Arrangements and Passing and Reincarnation of the 10th Panchen Lama), 30 Jan 1989
In 新时期宗教工作文献选编 (Collection of Literature on Religious Work in the New Era) (see below for book details)

制止和处理利用基督教进行非法违法活动 (Stopping and Dealing with Illegal Christian Activities), 18 Oct 1988
http://www.on118.com/LawDB/LawDetail.asp?ID=4271.

中华人民共和国海关对个人携带和邮寄印刷品进出境管理规定 (PRC Customs Provisions About the Management of Personally Carrying or Mailing Printed Materials In and Out of the Borders), 15 Jun 1988
See Articles 4 and 5. In 大陆地区宗教法规彙编 (Edited Religious Regulations of the Mainland) (see below for book details)

如何对待台湾宗教、会道门、帮会等人员来大陆探亲旅游问题 (How to Deal with Taiwanese Religious Personnel, Members of Sects and Secret Societies Traveling to Visit Relatives on the Mainland), 9 Jun 1988
http://www.on118.com/LawDB/LawDetail.asp?ID=4073.

中华人民共和国治安管理处罚条例 (节录) (Selections from the PRC Public Order Management and Punishment Regulation), 5 Sep 1986; amended 12 May 1994
See Articles 2, 19, 24, and 25 (particularly 24.4. In 大陆地区宗教法规彙编 (Edited Religious Regulations of the Mainland); also in 新时期民族宗教工作宣传手册 (Propaganda Handbook on Nationality and Religious Work) (see below for book details)

«中华人民共和国民法通则»第七十七条 (Article 77 of "General Rules of the PRC Civil Law"), 12 Apr 1986
Article 77 notes that associations (including religious associations) are protected by law. In 新时期宗教工作文献选编 (Collection of Literature on Religious Work in the New Era) (see below for book details)

中华人民共和国民法通则 (节录) (Selections from the PRC Civil Law), 12 Apr 1986
Relevant Article: 77. In 新时期民族宗教工作宣传手册 (Propaganda Handbook on Nationality and Religious Work) (see below for book details)

中华人民共和国义务教育法 (节录) (Selections from the PRC Compulsory Education Law), 12 Apr 1986
Relevant Articles are 4, 5, 16. In 新时期民族宗教工作宣传手册 (Propaganda Handbook on Nationality and Religious Work) (see below for book details)

中华人民共和国民族区域自治法关于宗教的规定 (Provisions of the PRC Regional Autonomy Law Related to Religion), 31 May 1984
See Articles 41 and 53. In 大陆地区宗教法规彙编 (Edited Mainland Religious Regulations) (see above for book details)

不作为宗教活动场所的寺观教堂等古建筑不得从事宗教和迷信活动 (Churches, Temples, Religious Venues, or Other Ancient Buildings Not in Use Are Not to Be Used for Religious or Superstitious Activities), 18 Jan 1984
http://www.makuielys.info/_private/law/mixing.htm.

关于确定汉族地区佛道教全国重点寺观的报告的通知 (Report on Determining the Key Buddhist and Daoist Monasteries of the Han Nationality Regions), 9 Apr 1983.

In 新时期宗教工作文献选编 (Collection of Literature on Religious Work in the New Era) or 新时期民族宗教工作宣传手册 (Propaganda Handbook on Nationality and Religious Work) (see below for book details); also at http://www.miaoyin.net/zhengcefagui/guanyuquedinhanzudequfodaoquanguozhongdiansiguandebaogao.htm.

中华人民共和国全国人民代表大会和地方各级人民代表大会选举法 (节录) (Selections from the PRC National People's Congress and People's Congresses of All Levels Election Law), 10 Dec 1982
See Article 2. In 新时期民族宗教工作宣传手册 (Propaganda Handbook on Nationality and Religious Work) (see below for book details)

寺庙、道观房屋产权归属问题的复函 (Reply Letter on Issues Related to Property Rights and Ownership of Temples and Daoist Monasteries), 27 Jan 1981
http://law.chinalawinfo.com/newlaw2002/SLC/SLC.asp?Db=chl&Gid=887.

落实宗教团体房产政策等问题 (Report on the Implementation of the Policy of Building Properties of Religious Groups and Other Issues), 3 Jul 1980.
Written by the Committee on Legal Work of the Standing Committee of the National People's Congress, this document aims to remedy the wrongs of the Cultural Revolution without seeming like the State itself was operating churches or religious venues and also avoid discriminating against religious ownership. Buildings owned before the Cultural Revolution should be returned, contracts reinstated, and frozen funds returned. The document can be found in 新时期民族宗教工作宣传手册 (Propaganda Handbook on Nationality and Religious Work) (see below for book details); the Chinese version can also be found online at http://www.on118.com/LawDB/LawDetail.asp?ID=1240.
An English translation is available at "Report on the Implementation of the Policy of Building Properties of Religious Groups and Other Issues," *Chinese Law and Government* 33, no. 2 (Mar/Apr 2000), 12–16.

中华人民共和国刑法 (节录) (Selections from the PRC Criminal Law), 1 Jul 1979; amended 24 Mar 1997
Relevant provisions include Article 251 (depriving citizen of freedom of religious belief carries up to a two-year penalty) and Article 300 (prohibiting using superstitious sects or cult organizations to undermine enforcement of laws). The Chinese version is 新时期民族宗教工作宣传手册 (Propaganda Handbook on Nationality and Religious Work) (see below for book details). English translations of the Criminal Code are available in many locations, including http://www.qis.net/chinalaw/prclaw60.htm.

关于"伊斯兰教"名称问题的通知 (Notice on Questions on the Name "Islam"), 2 Jun 1956. This regulation describes how the Chinese term 伊斯兰教 should be used instead of 回教 to refer to Islam.
http://www.ctnews.com.cn/webpub/template/aTpldef.asp?ID=3437&Cn=%D7%DA%BD%CC%B9%E6%B7%B6.

Regional Regulations

These regulations are organized by province (English alphabetical order); includes counties and cities within the respective provinces. Within provinces, the regulations are arranged in reverse chronological order, regardless of administrative level.

Anhui

蚌埠市宗教事务局 职能配置、内设机构和人员编制规定 (Bangbu City: Establishing Regulations on Functions, Assignments, Internal Organization, and Personnel of the Religious Affairs Bureau), 14 May 2002. http://www.bengbu.gov.cn/zfgw/020625-6.htm.

安徽省宗教事务条例 (Anhui Province: Religious Affairs Regulations), 15 Oct 1999. http://www.zytzb.org.cn/zytzbwz/flfg/zj5aa.htm.

安徽省宗教活动场所管理实施办法 (Anhui Province: Measures for Implementing the Management of Venues of Religious Activities), 15 Nov 1994. http://www.zytzb.org.cn/zytzbwz/flfg/zj8aj.htm.

安徽省关于进一步落实宗教团体房产政策的意见 (Anhui Province: Ideas on Further Implementing the Religious Group Real Estate Policy), 5 Nov 1984. http://www.e56.com.cn/minzu/autonomy/Law_detail.asp?Law_ID=43.

Beijing

北京市宗教事务条例 (Beijing Municipality: Religious Affairs Regulations), 18 Jul 2002. http://www.beijing.org.cn/3925/2002-8-7/182@363304.htm. An English translation is available in "Five Provincial Level Official Regulations on Religious Affairs," *Chinese Law and Government* 36, no. 3 (May–June 2003): 49–54.

Chongqing

重庆市宗教事务管理条例 (Chongqing Municipality: Regulations for the Management of Religious Affairs), 17 Oct 1997. http://www.zytzb.org.cn/zytzbwz/flfg/zj5ap.htm.

Fujian

福鼎市依法加强宗教事务管理深入开展宗教问题专项治理 (Fuding City: Legally Strengthening the Management of Religious Affairs and Thoroughly Carrying Out the Administration of Special Religious Issues), Mar 2001.

福建省宗教活动场所登记管理暂行规定 (Fujian Province Temporary Provisions for the Management of Registration of Venues of Religious Activities), 11 Sep 1992.

Chinese version at http://www.on118.com/LawDB/LawDetail.asp?ID=16553. English translation available in *Chinese Law and Government* 33, no. 3 (May–June 2000): 30–33.

厦门市宗教活动场所管理规定 (Xiamen City Provisions for the Management of Venues of Religious Activities), 13 Jan 2000.
http://www.on118.com/LawDB/LawDetail.asp?ID=17324.

Gansu
甘肃省宗教事务管理暂行规定 (Gansu Province: Temporary Provisions for Management of Religious Affairs), 16 Nov 1991.
http://www.zytzb.org.cn/zytzbwz/flfg/zj6af.htm.

兰州市宗教活动场所管理办法 (Lanzhou City Measures for the Management of Venues of Religious Activities), 25 Nov 1996. http://www.lz.gansu.gov.cn/zfjg/mwzjj.htm

Guangdong
广东省宗教事务管理条例 (Guangdong Province: Regulations for the Management of Religious Affairs), 30 Jun 2000. http://www.zytzb.org.cn/zytzbwz/flfg/zj5ab.htm. An English translation is available at "Five Provincial Level Official Regulations on Religious Affairs," *Chinese Law and Government* 36, no. 3 (May–June 2003): 60–68.

深圳经济特区宗教事务条例 (Shenzhen Special Economic Zone: Religious Affairs Regulations), 27 Oct 1998. http://www.zytzb.org.cn/zytzbwz/flfg/zj5am.htm.

广州市宗教事务管理条例 (Guangzhou City: Regulations for the Management of Religious Affairs), 26 Sep 1997.
Chinese version available at http://www.zytzb.org.cn/zytzbwz/flfg/zj5ac.htm.
English translation available in *Chinese Law and Government* 33, no. 3 (May–June 2000): 17–26; also in Human Rights Watch, *State Control of Religion: Update Number 1* (1999).

关于制止乱建寺庙的意见 (Ideas on Stopping the Random Construction of Temples and Monasteries), 7 Oct 1996.
http://www.e56.com.cn/minzu/autonomy/Law_detail.asp?Law_ID=129.

宗教团体规章制度 (Religious Groups Rules and Regulations), Mar 1994
Issued by the Guangdong Province RAB, this ninety-page document describes the internal regulations of each of the eight religious associations in Guangdong Province.

广东省宗教活动场所行政管理规定 (Guangdong Province: Provisions on the Administration and Management of Venues of Religious Activities), 23 Mar 1988.
Chinese version available at http://www.zytzb.org.cn/zytzbwz/flfg/zj8am.htm.

English translations available in Asia Division of Human Rights Watch, *Freedom of Religion in China* (New York: Human Rights, January 1992): 60–63; *Chinese Law and Government* 33, no. 3 (May–June 2000): 12–16.

佛山市宗教活动场所行政管理暂定规定 (Foshan City: Temporary Provisions on the Administration and Management of Venues of Religious Activities), 15 Oct 1987.
In 大陆地区宗教法规彙编 (Edited Mainland Religious Regulations) (see below for book details)

广州市宗教事务行政管理暂行规定 (Guangzhou City Temporary Provisions for the Management of Religious Affairs), 3 Apr 1987.
http://www.zytzb.org.cn/zytzbwz/flfg/zj6ah.htm.

广东省关于落实宗教团体房产政策问题的报告 (Guangdong Province: Report on Implementing the Religious Group Real Estate Policy), 4 Mar 1981.
http://www.e56.com.cn/minzu/autonomy/Law_detail.asp?Law_ID=44.

Guangxi

广西壮族自治区宗教事务行政管理暂行规定 (Guangxi Zhuang Nationality Autonomous Region: Temporary Administrative Provisions for the Management of Religious Affairs), 22 Mar 1994. Published in *Guangxi Ribao*, May 2, 1994. Also at http://www.zytzb.org.cn/zytzbwz/flfg/zj6ac.htm.

当前我区宗教工作的几点 (Guangxi Region: Several Points about Current Religious Work in Guangxi Region), 31 Jan 1989.
http://www.e56.com.cn/minzu/autonomy/Law_detail.asp?Law_ID=52.

进一步落实宗教团体房产政策的意见 (Guangxi Region: Ideas on Further Implementing the Religious Groups Real Estate Policy), 6 Jan 1986.
http://www.e56.com.cn/minzu/autonomy/Law_detail.asp?Law_ID=132.

Guizhou

贵州省宗教事务管理条例 (Guizhou Province Regulations for the Management of Religious Affairs), 22 Jul 2000. http://www.zytzb.org.cn/zytzbwz/flfg/zj5ad.htm.

贵州省宗教活动场所管理办法 (Guizhou Province: Measures for the Management of Venues of Religious Activities), 24 Dec 1992.
http://www.zytzb.org.cn/zytzbwz/flfg/zj8ao.htm.

Hainan

海南省宗教事务管理条例 (Hainan Province: Regulations for the Management of Religious Affairs), 26 Sep 1997. http://www.zytzb.org.cn/zytzbwz/flfg/zj5ae.htm.

Hebei

河北省保障天主教正常宗教活动的规定（试行）(Hebei Province: Provisions to Safeguard the Normal Religious Activities of the Catholic Church (implementation)), 13 May 1989. http://www.zytzb.org.cn/zytzbwz/flfg/zj8ac.htm.

Heilongjiang

黑龙江省宗教事务管理条例 (Heilongjiang Province: Regulations for the Management of Religious Affairs), 12 Jun 1997. http://www.zytzb.org.cn/zytzbwz/flfg/zj5af.htm.

Henan

河南省宗教活动场所管理办法（试行）(Henan Province: Measures for the Management of Venues of Religious Activities (implementation)), 21 Aug 1991.
Chinese version at http://www.zytzb.org.cn/zytzbwz/flfg/zj7ac.htm. English translation available in *Chinese Law and Government* 33, no. 3 (May–June 2000): 78–82.

Hubei

湖北省宗教事务管理条例 (Hubei Province: Regulations for the Management of Religious Affairs), 14 Jan 2001.
http://law.sdinfo.net/77407839378735104/20010114/177369.shtml.

湖北省宗教事务管理暂行规定 (Hubei Province: Temporary Provisions for the Management of Religious Affairs), 29 Oct 1992 (amended 1 Jan 1998).
http://www.zytzb.org.cn/zytzbwz/flfg/zj6ab.htm.

武汉市宗教活动场所管理办法 (Wuhan City: Measures for the Management of Venues of Religious Activities), 21 Jul 1994. http://www.zytzb.org.cn/zytzbwz/flfg/zj7af.htm.

Hunan

湖南省宗教事务管理条例 (Hunan Province: Regulations for the Management of Religious Affairs), 28 Sep 2000. http://zjsw.hunan.gov.cn/txt/fg07.htm.

湖南省实施〈宗教活动场所管理条例〉办法 (Hunan Province: Measures Implementing "Regulations for the Management of Venues of Religious Activities" [Decree 145]), 30 Dec 1997. http://zjsw.hunan.gov.cn/txt/fg08.htm.

湖南省实施《宗教活动场所管理条例》办法 (Hunan Province: Measures Implementing "Regulations for the Management of Venues of Religious Activities" [Decree 145]), 14 Dec 1995. http://www.zytzb.org.cn/zytzbwz/flfg/zj8al.htm.

Jiangsu

江苏省宗教事务条例 (Jiangsu Province: Religious Affairs Regulations), 5 Feb 2002. http://www.fowang.org/zongjiaozhengce/new_page_715.htm. An English translation is available at "Five Provincial Level Official Regulations on Religious Affairs," *Chinese Law and Government* 36, no. 3 (May–June 2003): 68–74.

江苏省实施《宗教活动场所管理条例》办法 (Jiangsu Province: Measures for Implementing "Regulations for the Management of Venues of Religious Activities" [Decree 145]), 9 Oct 1998. http://www.zytzb.org.cn/zytzbwz/flfg/zj8ah.htm.

Jiangxi

江西省宗教事务管理办法 (Jiangxi Province Measures for the Regulation of Religious Affairs), 5 Jan 1998. http://www.zytzb.org.cn/zytzbwz/flfg/zj6aa.htm.

Jilin

吉林省宗教事务条例 (Jilin Province: Religious Affairs Regulations), 19 Dec 1997. http://www.zytzb.org.cn/zytzbwz/flfg/zj5ah.htm.

Liaoning

辽宁省宗教事务管理条例 (Liaoning Province: Regulations for the Management of Religious Affairs), 28 Nov 1998. http://www.zytzb.org.cn/zytzbwz/flfg/zj5ai.htm. An English translation is available at "Five Provincial Level Official Regulations on Religious Affairs," *Chinese Law and Government* 36, no. 3 (May–June 2003): 74–80.

辽宁省宗教活动场所管理规定 (Liaoning Province Provisions for the Management of Venues of Religious Activities), 12 Nov 1993. http://www.zytzb.org.cn/zytzbwz/flfg/zj8ae.htm.

Nei Mengu (Inner Mongolia)

内蒙古自治区宗教活动场所管理实施办法 (Nei Mongu [Inner Mongolia] Autonomous Region: Measures for Implementing the Management of Venues of Religious Activities), 23 Jan 1996. http://www.zytzb.org.cn/zytzbwz/flfg/zj8ad.htm.

Ningxia

宁夏回族自治区宗教事务管理暂行规定 (Ningxia Autonomous Region Temporary Provisions for the Management of Religious Affairs), 7 Jun 1994. http://www.zytzb.org.cn/zytzbwz/flfg/zj6ag.htm.

Qinghai

青海省宗教教职人员管理规定 (Qinghai Province: Provisions for the Management of Religious Personnel), 28 Aug 1992.
Chinese version at http://www.zytzb.org.cn/zytzbwz/flfg/zj7ae.htm. English translation available in *Chinese Law and Government* 33, no. 3 (May–June 2000): 87–89.

青海省宗教活动场所管理规定 (Qinghai Province: Provisions for the Management of Venues of Religious Activities), 28 Aug 1992.
http://www.zytzb.org.cn/zytzbwz/flfg/zj7ad.htm. English translation available in *Chinese Law and Government* 33, no. 3 (May–June 2000): 83–86.

Shaanxi

陕西省宗教事务条例 (Shaanxi Province: Religious Affairs Regulations), 23 Sep 2000.
http://www.zytzb.org.cn/zytzbwz/flfg/zj5ak.htm.

陕西省实施《宗教活动场所管理条例》办法 (Shaanxi Province: Measures Implementing "Regulations for the Management of Venues of Religious Activities" [Decree 145]), http://www.zytzb.org.cn/zytzbwz/flfg/zj8ap.htm.

陕西省关于外国旅游者到宗教活动场所从事宗教活动的暂行规定 (Shaanxi Province: Temporary Provisions Regarding Foreign Travelers to Venues of Religious Activities to Engage in Religious Activities), 18 May 1992.
http://www.zytzb.org.cn/zytzbwz/flfg/zj8aq.htm.

Shandong

济南市宗教事务管理条例 (Jinan City: Regulations for the Management of Religious Affairs), 29 Sep 2000. http://www.jinan.gov.cn/zcfg/ViewLawsRegulations.asp?key=103.

山东省宗教事务管理条例 (Shandong Province: Regulations for the Management of Religious Affairs), 25 Aug 2000. http://www.zytzb.org.cn/zytzbwz/flfg/zj5aj.htm.

青岛市: 关于对本市土地使用权出让转让和城市房屋改造中涉及宗教房地产 (Qingdao City: Regarding the Power to Use, Sell, and Transfer Civic Buildings and Religious Real Estate in the City), 13 Feb 1996.
http://www.e56.com.cn/minzu/autonomy/Law_detail.asp?Law_ID=100.

山东省宗教活动场所管理办法 (Shandong Province: Measures for the Management of Venues of Religious Activities), 18 Nov 1993.
Chinese version at http://www.zytzb.org.cn/zytzbwz/flfg/zj7ab.htm. English translation available in *Chinese Law and Government* 33, no. 3 (May–June 2000): 69–73.

关于落实宗教团体房产政策情况和意见的报告 (Report on Ideas and the Situation on Implementing the Religious Group Real Estate Policy), 13 Feb 1982. http://www.e56.com.cn/minzu/autonomy/Law_detail.asp?Law_ID=99.

Shanghai

上海市宗教事务条例 (Shanghai Municipality: Religious Affairs Regulations), 30 Nov 1995.

This regulation, along with the one below, formed the basis for many other regulations after provincial leaders came to Shanghai for a religious work conference to learn about the success of the regulation in Shanghai. The Chinese version is available at http://www.zytzb.org.cn/zytzbwz/flfg/zj5al.htm. An English translation by *Tripod* is available at http://www.hrw.org/reports/1997/china1/.

上海市宗教活动场所管理规定 (Shanghai Municipality: Provisions for the Management of Venues of Religious Activities), 15 May 1995. http://www.zytzb.org.cn/zytzbwz/flfg/zj8af.htm.

上海市宗教印制品管理办法 (Shanghai Municipality: Measures for the Management of Religious Printings), 31 Dec 1997. http://mzw.sh.gov.cn/gb/mzw/zwgk/zcfg/userobject1ai280.html.

Shanxi

[no extant regulations available as of this writing]

Sichuan

四川省宗教事务管理条例 (Sichuan Province: Regulations for the Management of Religious Affairs), 9 May 2000. http://www.zytzb.org.cn/zytzbwz/flfg/zj5an.htm.

成都市宗教活动场所管理办法 (Chengdu City: Measures for the Management of Venues of Religious Activities), 26 Jul 1995. http://www.zytzb.org.cn/zytzbwz/flfg/zj7ag.htm.

四川省宗教教职人员管理规定 (Sichuan Province Provisions for the Management of Religious Personnel), 20 Oct 1993. http://www.zytzb.org.cn/zytzbwz/flfg/zj8an.htm.

Tianjin

天津市宗教教职人员活动管理办法 (Tianjin Municipality: Measures for the Management of Religious Personnel), 9 Oct 1997. http://www.zytzb.org.cn/zytzbwz/flfg/zj8aa.htm.

天津市宗教活动场所管理办法 (Tianjin Municipality: Measures for the Management of Venues of Religious Activities), 21 Feb 1994. http://www.zytzb.org.cn/zytzbwz/flfg/zj7aa.htm.

Xinjiang

新疆维吾尔自治区宗教事务管理条例 (Xinjiang Uygur Autonomous Region: Regulations for the Management of Religious Affairs), 16 Jul 1994. http://www.e56.com.cn/minzu/autonomy/Law_detail.asp?Law_ID=165.

新疆维吾尔自治区宗教活动管理暂行规定 (Xinjiang Uygur Autonomous Region: Temporary Provisions for the Management of Religious Activities), 23 Aug 1990. http://www.zytzb.org.cn/zytzbwz/flfg/zj8as.htm. English translation available in Asia Division of Human Rights Watch, *Freedom of Religion in China*: 64–67 (see below for book details); *Chinese Law and Government* 33, no. 3 (May–June 2000): 90–93.

新疆维吾尔自治区宗教职业人员管理暂行规定 (Xinjiang Uygur Autonomous Region: Temporary Provisions for the Management of Religious Professional Personnel), 23 Aug 1990. http://www.zytzb.org.cn/zytzbwz/flfg/zj8ar.htm.

自治区人大常委会关于自治区人民政府宗教工作情况报告的决议 (Standing Committee of the People's Congress of the Autonomous Region: Resolution on the People's Government Status Report of Religious Work in the Autonomous Region (12 May 1990) In 大陆地区宗教法规彙编 (Edited Religious Regulations of the Mainland) (see below for book details)

新疆维吾尔自治区宗教活动场所管理暂行规则 (Xinjiang Uygur Autonomous Region: Temporary Rules for the Management of Venues of Religious Activities), 12 May 1988. http://www.zytzb.org.cn/zytzbwz/flfg/zj8at.htm.

Xizang (Tibet)

西藏自治区宗教事务管理暂行办法 (Xizang [Tibet] Autonomous Region: Temporary Measures for the Management of Religious Affairs), 9 Dec 1991. http://www.zytzb.org.cn/zytzbwz/flfg/zj6ae.htm.

Yunnan

昆明市宗教活动场所管理条例 (Kunming City: Regulations for the Management of Venues of Religious Activities), 28 Nov 1998. http://www.zytzb.org.cn/zytzbwz/flfg/zj7ah.htm.

云南省宗教事务管理规定 (Yunnan Province: Provisions for the Management of Religious Affairs), 25 Dec 1997. http://www.zytzb.org.cn/zytzbwz/flfg/zj6ad.htm.

Zhejiang

浙江省宗教事务条例 (Zhejiang Province: Religious Affairs Regulations), 9 May 2000. http://www.zytzb.org.cn/zytzbwz/flfg/zj5ao.htm.

浙江省宗教事务条例 (Zhejiang Province: Religious Affairs Regulations), 11 Dec 1997. http://www.people.com.cn/item/flfgk/dffg/1997/C411086199701.html.

宁波市宗教活动场所管理办法 (Ningbo City: Measures for the Management of Venues of Religious Activities), 27 Mar 1997. http://www.zytzb.org.cn/zytzbwz/flfg/zj7ai.htm.

浙江省宗教活动管理规定 (Zhejiang Province: Provisions for the Management of Religious Activities), 16 Apr 1992. http://www.zytzb.org.cn/zytzbwz/flfg/zj8ai.htm.

Government and Party Documents, Notices, and Decisions

關于進一步加強馬克思无神論研究和宣傳教育工作的通知 Notice on Further Strengthening Marxist Atheism research, Propaganda and Education (May 28, 2004). Issued by the Department of Propaganda of the Central Committee of CPC No. (2004) 13. This secret document is the Party's response to the rapid development of religion, which may pose a threat to the Party. For full text: http://www.chinaaid.org/English/news-english.htm

关于填报 «聘请外国文教专家单位资格认可申请表» 有关问题的意见 Opinions and Questions Regarding How to Fill in the Form "Inviting Foreign Cultural and Education Experts Approval Request (21 Jan 1999)
Issued by SARA, this sixteen-page document includes the following: (1) the cover sheet that accompanies national regulations sent to the provincial levels, (2) the document "Opinions and Questions Regarding How to Fill in the Form 'Inviting Foreign Cultural and Education Experts Approval Request Form,'" (3) the form 'Inviting Foreign Cultural and Education Experts Approval Request Form,' (4) a chart: Foreign Expert Job Management Organization and Personnel Situation, (5) another chart: Living Funds and Economic Collection Situation, (6) a "Notice of Questions Related to 'Hiring Foreign Specialists at Religious Colleges and Universities for Short-term Lectures Requires Written Notice,'" (7) the approval certificate.

宗教院校聘用外籍专业人员办法 Measures for Hiring Foreign Specialists at Religious Colleges and Universities (22 Jan 1999)
Issued by SARA, the first two pages are the cover sheet that accompanies national regulations sent to the provincial levels; the remainder are instructions on how to interpret and implement the regulations.

中国的宗教信仰自由状况 Freedom of Religious Belief in China (17 Oct 1997)
This document was published by the Information Office of the State Council of the People's Republic of China. It is the official statement of Chinese religious policy. The document is available at many Internet sites, including the United Front web site: http://www.zytzb.org.cn/zytzbwz/flfg/zj2.htm. An English translation is available both in booklet form and at http://www.humanrights-china.org/whitepapers/white_c11.htm.

中国现今的宗教问题: 再次探讨宗教的五性 China's Current Religious Question: Once Again an Inquiry into the Five Characteristics of Religion (22 Mar 1996)
Written by Ye Xiaowen, currently the director-general of SARA; found in *Selections of Reports of the Party School of the Central Committee of the Chinese Communist Party*, no. 5 (1996).

认真做好宗教活动场所登记工作 Conscientiously Do a Good Job at Registering Venues of Religious Activity (21 Sep 1994)
Issued by SARA. In 大陆地区宗教法规彙编 (Edited Mainland Religious Regulations) (see above for book details)

外国人宗教活动管理规定若干条款的解释 Explanation of Certain Provisions in the Provisions for Management of Foreigners' Religious Activities (29 Jun 1994)
Issued by SARA. In 大陆地区宗教法规彙编 (Edited Mainland Religious Regulations) (see above for book details)

新闻出版署关于全面检查涉及伊斯兰教的出版物的通知 Notice of the Press and Publications Office Regarding Examining Every Facet Involved in Islamic Publications (1993)
In 新时期民族宗教工作宣传手册 (Propaganda Handbook on Nationality and Religious Work) (see below for book details)

附录二: 宗教信仰自由: 国务院新闻办公室发布关于西藏问题的白皮书«西藏的主权归属与人权状况»第八部分 Appendix 2: Freedom of Religious Belief: State Council Press Office Releases Part Eight of a White Paper about the Xizang Issue: "The Condition of Xizang Sovereignty and Human Rights" (Sep 1992)
Xizang is commonly referred to as Tibet in the West. In 新时期宗教工作文献选编 (Collection of Literature on Religious Work in the New Era) (see below for book details)

公民享有宗教信仰自由: 国务院新闻办公室发布的 «中国的人权状况» 白皮书第六部分 Citizens Enjoy Freedom of Religious Belief: State Council Press Office Releases Part Six of the White Paper "Chinese Human Rights Condition" (Oct 1991)
Appendix 1 of 新时期宗教工作文献选编 (Collection of Literature on Religious Work in the New Era) (see below for book details)

关于制止一些地方利用宗教活动妨碍学校教育问题的通知 Notice on Stopping the Exploitation of Religious Activities to Hinder Schools and Education in Several Regions (5 Aug 1991)
In 大陆地区宗教法规彙编 (Edited Religious Regulations of the Mainland) (see above for book details)

中共中央国务院关于进一步做好宗教工作若干问题的通知 (Document No. 6: Circular Issued by the Central Committee of the Communist Party and the State Council on Some Problems Concerning Further Improving Work on Religion), 5 Feb 1991.
This internal party document notes the use of religion as a tool for infiltration and peaceful evolution, and seeks to tighten state control of religion, especially with regard to foreign contacts, to prevent infiltration and peaceful evolution. The document can be found in In 新时期宗教工作文献选编 (Collection of Literature on Religious Work in the New Era) (see below for book details), or online at http://chinacatholic.org/LAW/Law011.htm; an English translation can be found in Asia Watch, *Freedom of Religion in China* (1992), 30–35 [listed in the "Books in English" section above].

中共中央组织部关于妥善解决共产党员信仰宗教问题的通知 Circular Concerning the Appropriate Resolution of the Issue of Communist Party Members Believing in Religions (28 Jan 1991)
Written by the Organization Department of the Central Committee of the CCP, this circular discusses how Party members should be nonbelievers: those who have participated in religious should be persuaded to stop or withdraw from the party. Exceptions are made for national minority cadres who may "participate in activities that pertain purely to ethnic customs." This document can be found in 新时期宗教工作文献选编 (Collection of Literature on Religious Work in the New Era) (see below for book details); in 新时期民族宗教工作宣传手册 (Propaganda Handbook on Nationality and Religious Work) (see below for book details); and *Xinxi Shenzhou* [My Heart is Bound to China], *Fuyin Zhengzhuhui* [Bible Witness Association], 148–50. An English translation is available: "Circular Concerning the Appropriate Resolution of the Issue of Communist Party Members Believing in Religions," *Chinese Law and Government* 33, no. 2 (Mar/Apr 2000), 46–48.

巩固和扩大党同各民族爱国宗教界的统一战线: «中共中央关于加强统一战线工作的通知» 的一部分 Consolidating and Expanding the Party's United Front on All Nationality and Religious Circles: Part of "Notice of the CPC Central Committee Strengthening the United Front Work" (14 Jul 1990)
This document, issued by the CPC Central Committee, focuses on the importance of atheistic education and that religion should be adapted to fit within the socialist system. In 新时期宗教工作文献选编 (Collection of Literature on Religious Work in the New Era) (see below for book details); also in 中国大陆研究 (*Mainland China Studies*) 36, no. 5 (May 1993), 104–111.

接待台胞中的宗教人士应注意哪些问题 (Which Issues Those Who Admit Taiwanese Religious Figures Should Pay Attention to) (Jun 1992)
Issued by the Shanghai City Taiwan Affairs Office. In 大陆地区宗教法规彙编 (Edited Mainland Religious Regulations) (see above for book details)

关于宗教方面对台交往的规定 (Provisions on the Religious Aspect of Associations with Taiwan (May 1990)
Issued by the CCP 中华全国台湾同胞联谊会宣传部. In 大陆地区宗教法规彙编 (Edited Mainland Religious Regulations) (see above for book details)

中央办公厅文件:关于在新形势下,加强天主教工作的报告 Document No. 3: Stepping up Control over the Catholic Church to Meet the New Situation (1989)
In 中央与梵蒂岗关系 (Central Committee–Vatican Relations), page 540.

新闻出版署关于认真检查涉及民族，宗教问题书刊的通知 Notice of the Press and Publications Office Regarding Conscientiously Examining Nationality and Religious Issues Involved in Books and Periodicals (10 May 1989)
In 新时期民族宗教工作宣传手册 (Propaganda Handbook on Nationality and Religious Work) (see below for book details)

中共中央统战部关于建议为全国统战,民族,宗教工作部门摘掉 "执行投降主义路线" 帽子的请示报告 CPC United Front Department Report Recommending that the Entire Country's United Front, Nationalities, and Religion Work Departments Cast Aside the "Execute the Surrenderist Path" Label (3 Feb 1989).
The "surrenderist" label denoted those who did not fully follow orders or who are "defeatist." In 新时期宗教工作文献选编 (Collection of Literature on Religious Work in the New Era) (see below for book details)

关于妥善处理军队住用宗教团体的房产权属问题: «国务院,中央军委关于妥善处理军队与地方部分房地产权属问题的通知» 第五点 Carefully and Skillfully Dealing with the Jurisdictional Issue of the Military's Use of Religious Groups' Land: Point Five of "Notice of the State Council and Central Military Commission About Carefully and Skillfully Dealing with the Military and Local Departments Separating Real Estate and Jurisdictional Issues (18 Jul 1988)
In 新时期宗教工作文献选编 (Collection of Literature on Religious Work in the New Era) (see below for book details).

中央宣传部关于印发«对宣传教育工作中涉及宗教问题的一些意见»的通知 Notice of the Central Propaganda Department's Distribution of "Some Ideas about Religious Issues Involved in Education Propaganda Work" (28 Feb 1986)
In 新时期民族宗教工作宣传手册 (Propaganda Handbook on Nationality and Religious Work) (see below for book details)

中共中央办公厅,国务院办公厅转发中央办公厅调查组«关于落实党的宗教政策及有关问题的调查报告»的通知 Notice on the CPC Central Committee Office and State Council Office Forwarding the Central Office Research Unit's "Survey Report Concerning the Implementation of the Party's Policies on Religion and Relevant Issues" (29 Dec 1985)
Written by the Survey Team of the General Office of the Central Committee of the Chinese Communist Party, this document analyzes the importance of correctly managing Buddhist monasteries and Daoist temples. In 新时期宗教工作文献选编 (Collection of Literature on Religious Work in the New Era; see below for book details); and at http://www.on118.com/LawDB/LawDetail.asp?ID=2933. An English translation is available at "Survey Report Concerning the Implementation of the Party's Policies on Religion and Relevant Issues," *Chinese Law and Government* 33, no. 2 (Mar/Apr 2000), 35–45.

重视研究统一战线和民族,宗教问题: «中共中央统战部关于全国统一战线理论工作会议的情况报告» 的一部分 Attach Importance to Researching the United Front and Nationality and Religious Issues: Part of "Status Report of the CPC Central Committee United Front Department on the Theory and Work Conference" (9 Jun 1985)
In 新时期宗教工作文献选编 (Collection of Literature on Religious Work in the New Era) (see below for book details)

中央统战部关于公开发行的书籍报刊中慎重对待民族，宗教问题的通知 Notice of the United Front Department Regarding Carefully Approaching Nationality and Religion Questions in Publicly Published Books, Newspapers, and Magazines (23 Mar 1985)
In 新时期民族宗教工作宣传手册 (Propaganda Handbook on Nationality and Religious Work) (see below for book details)

香港特别行政区居民的权利和自由: «中华人民共和国政府对香港的基本方针政策的具体说明»的一部分 Hong Kong Special Administrative Region Residents' Rights and Freedoms: Part of "Comprehensive Explanation of Basic Principles and Policy of the PRC Toward Hong Kong" (19 Dec 1984)
In 新时期宗教工作文献选编 (Collection of Literature on Religious Work in the New Era) (see below for book details)

中共中央关于印发«西藏工作座谈会纪要»的通知 Notice of the Central Committee of the CPC Printing "Summary of Xizang Work Forum" (1 Apr 1984)
In 新时期宗教工作文献选编 (Collection of Literature on Religious Work in the New Era) (see below for book details)

中共中央关于在清除精神污染中正确对待宗教问题的指示 CPC Central Committee: Instructions on Eliminating Spiritual Pollution in Handling Religious Issues (11 Dec 1983)
In 新时期宗教工作文献选编 (Collection of Literature on Religious Work in the New Era) (see below for book details)

发扬中国佛教优良的传统，为四化建设做出更大贡献 Developing the Good Traditions of Chinese Buddhism, to Make an Even Greater Contribution to the Four Modernizations (7 Dec 1983)
In 新时期宗教工作文献选编 (Collection of Literature on Religious Work in the New Era) (see below for book details)

教育部，国家民委，国务院宗教事务局转发甘肃省康乐县关于«在普及小学教育中注意发挥宗教界人士的积极作用»的通知 Education Bureau, State Nationalities Committee, State Administration for Religious Affairs [SARA] Forwards Gansu Province Kangle County's Notice: "In Elementary Education, Pay Attention to the Positive Role Models of People of Religious Walks of Life" (18 Jul 1983)
In 新时期宗教工作文献选编 (Collection of Literature on Religious Work in the New Era) (see below for book details)

社会主义时期宗教问题的基本观点和基本政策 (Document No. 19: The Basic Viewpoint on the Religious Question During Our Country's Socialist Period), 31 Mar 1982.
This policy document, issued by the CPC Central Committee, is the foundation document for post-Mao religious policy. The document lays out the Party's long-term strategy for dealing with religion: prevent religion from spreading, but use law to protect freedom of religious belief (and non-belief). The document also acknowledges "leftist" errors ("左"的错误) in dealing with religion in the past. It stresses the five "natures" of religion and the necessity of using patriotic religious associations coordinated by the United Front. An English translation can be found in Donald MacInnis, *Religion in China Today: Policy and Practice* (Maryknoll: Orbis Books, 1989); the translation is reprinted in *Asia Watch, Freedom of Religion in China* (1992), 30–35; and in R. Lanier Britsch, "The Current Legal Status of Christianity in China," 1995 *BYU Law Review* 364–383 (1995).

要继续贯彻执行宗教信仰自由的政策：摘自«中国共产党中央委员会关于建国以来党的若干历史问题的决议» Continue to Effectuate and Execute the Policy of Freedom of Religious Belief: Selections from "CPC Central Committee Resolutions on Certain Historical Issues Since the Founding of the Nation" (27 Jun 1981)
In 新时期宗教工作文献选编 (Collection of Literature on Religious Work in the New Era) (see below for book details); also in 新时期民族宗教工作宣传手册 (Propaganda Handbook on Nationality and Religious Work) (see below for book details)

中共中央关于转发«西藏工作座谈会纪要» Central Committee of the CPC Forwards "Summary of Xizang Work Forum" (7 Apr 1980)
In 新时期宗教工作文献选编 (Collection of Literature on Religious Work in the New Era) (see below for book details)

新时期党的民族工作与宗教政策 The Party's Nationality Work and Religion Policy in the New Era (23 Sep 1979)

In 新时期宗教工作文献选编 (Collection of Literature on Religious Work in the New Era) (see below for book details)

Commentary and Policy Directives

朱镕基强调贯彻宗教信仰自由政策 (Zhu Rongji Emphasizes the Implementation of the Policy of Religious Freedom), 12 Jan 2003.
This is a speech given by former premier Zhu Rongji at a religious work meeting. http://www.people.com.cn/GB/shizheng/20030112/906124.html.

江泽民在全国宗教工作会议上发表重要讲话 (Jiang Zemin's Important Speech Given at a Nationwide Religious Work Conference), 11 Dec 2001.
Former President Jiang Zemin's speech at the nationwide religion conference set the tone for the current religious policy. The speech can be found at http://chinacatholic.org/LAW/news04.htm.

中国宗教的百年回顾与前瞻 One Hundred Years of Religion in China: Retrospective and Prospective (Ye Xiaowen) (19 Feb 2001).
Ye Xiaowen, the current director of SARA, spoke at the Chinese University of Hong Kong. He gave a broad retrospective on religion from the beginning of the twentieth century through liberation to the present. At http://www.china.org.cn/chinese/ch-zongjiao/index.htm. An English version is available at http://www.china.org.cn/english/features/45466.htm.

关于民族和宗教问题 (江泽民) Nationality and Religion Issues (Jiang Zemin) (20 Jul 1994)
In 新时期宗教工作文献选编 (Collection of Literature on Religious Work in the New Era) (see below for book details)

新形势下的民族宗教问题 (李瑞环) Issues under the New Nationality and Religion Situation (Li Ruihuan) (4 Jul 1994)
In 新时期宗教工作文献选编 (Collection of Literature on Religious Work in the New Era); also in 新时期民族宗教工作宣传手册 (Propaganda Handbook on Nationality and Religious Work) (see below for book details)

适应新形势的要求,开创宗教工作的新局面 (司马义▪艾买提) Adapt to the Requirements of the New Situation, Create a New Situation in Religious Work (Ismail Amat) (12 Jan 1994)
In 新时期宗教工作文献选编 (Collection of Literature on Religious Work in the New Era) (see below for book details)

充分发挥伊斯兰教协会的积极作用 (李瑞环) Fully Develop the Positive Role of the Chinese Islamic Association (Li Ruihuan) (17 Dec 1993)

In 新时期宗教工作文献选编 (Collection of Literature on Religious Work in the New Era) (see below for book details)

高度重视民族工作和宗教工作 (江泽民) Take Very Seriously Nationality and Religion Work (Jiang Zemin) (7 Nov 1993)
Speech given at the 1993 National United Front Work Conference: religion should reform its doctrine and practice to adapt itself to socialist society. In 新时期宗教工作文献选编 (Collection of Literature on Religious Work in the New Era); also in 新时期民族宗教工作宣传手册 (Propaganda Handbook on Nationality and Religious Work) (see below for book details)

发挥教特有优势,为建设伟大祖国做出贡献 (李瑞环) Develop Religion's Distinctive Superiority in Order to Make a Contribution Toward Building a Greater Motherland (Li Ruihuan) (21 Oct 1993)
In 新时期宗教工作文献选编 (Collection of Literature on Religious Work in the New Era) (see below for book details)

在全国性宗教团体领导人迎春座谈会上的谈话 (李瑞环) Statement Given at the Spring Welcoming National Conference for Religious Leaders (Li Ruihuan) (19 Jan 1993)
In 新时期宗教工作文献选编 (Collection of Literature on Religious Work in the New Era); also in 新时期民族宗教工作宣传手册 (Propaganda Handbook on Nationality and Religious Work) (see below for book details)

宗教界组织要引导信教群众爱教,爱国,爱社会主义 (宋平) Religious Circle Organizations Must Guide the Believing Masses to Love Religion, Love their Country, and Love Socialism (Song Ping) (15 Jun 1992)
In 新时期宗教工作文献选编 (Collection of Literature on Religious Work in the New Era) (see below for book details)

在全国宗教局长会议上的讲话 (陈俊生) Speech Given at the National Conference for Religious Chiefs (Chen Junsheng) (21 Feb 1992)
In 新时期宗教工作文献选编 (Collection of Literature on Religious Work in the New Era) (see below for book details)

关于宗教工作的问题 (李鹏) Issues Related to Religious Work (Li Peng) (18 Jan 1992)
In 新时期宗教工作文献选编 (Collection of Literature on Religious Work in the New Era); also in 新时期民族宗教工作宣传手册 (Propaganda Handbook on Nationality and Religious Work) (see below for book details)

党的宗教政策 (丁关根) The Party's Religious Policy (Ding Guangen) (29 Jun 1991)
In 新时期宗教工作文献选编 (Collection of Literature on Religious Work in the New Era) (see below for book details)

保持党的宗教政策的稳定性和连续性 (江泽民) Supporting the Stability and Continuity of the Party's Religious Policy (Jiang Zemin) (30 Jan 1991)
In 新时期宗教工作文献选编 (Collection of Literature on Religious Work in the New Era) (see below for book details)

一定要做好宗教工作 (江泽民) We Must Perform Religious Work Well (Jiang Zemin) (7 Dec 1990)
Speech given at the December 1990 Religious Work Conference. In 新时期宗教工作文献选编 (Collection of Literature on Religious Work in the New Era) (see below for book details)

进一步重视,关心和做好宗教工作 (李鹏) Attach Even More Importance, Pay Attention to, and Perform Well the Religious Work (Li Peng) (5 Dec 1990)
Speech given at the December 1990 Religious Work Conference. In 新时期宗教工作文献选编 (Collection of Literature on Religious Work in the New Era); also in 新时期民族宗教工作宣传手册 (Propaganda Handbook on Nationality and Religious Work) (see below for book details)

在中国天主教反帝爱国运动四十周年纪念会上的讲话 (吴学谦) Speech Given at the Fortieth Anniversary Commemoration of the Chinese Catholic Anti-Imperialist Patriotic Activity (Wu Xueqian) (30 Nov 1990)
In 新时期宗教工作文献选编 (Collection of Literature on Religious Work in the New Era) (see below for book details)

必须树立马克思主义的民族观和宗教观 (江泽民) The Necessity of Establishing the Marxist View of Nationalities and Religion (Jiang Zemin) (Sep 1990)
In 新时期宗教工作文献选编 (Collection of Literature on Religious Work in the New Era) (see below for book details)

关于高度重视宗教渗透问题的信 (陈云) A Message About Taking Very Seriously the Religious Infiltration Question (Chen Yun) (4 Apr 1990)
In 新时期宗教工作文献选编 (Collection of Literature on Religious Work in the New Era) (see below for book details)

班禅额尔德尼▪确吉坚赞副委员长永垂不朽 (万里) Eternal Glory to Assistant Committee Chair Panchen Erdeni Qoigyi Gyaincan (Wan Li) (15 Feb 1989)
In 新时期宗教工作文献选编 (Collection of Literature on Religious Work in the New Era) (see below for book details)

在纪念中国天主教自选自圣主教三十周年座谈会上的讲话 (吴学谦) Speech at the Chinese Catholic Self-Selected, Self-Ordained Bishops' Thirtieth Anniversary Forum (Wu Xueqian) (29 Nov 1988)
In 新时期宗教工作文献选编 (Collection of Literature on Religious Work in the New Era) (see below for book details)

在接见中国道教协会第四届会议代表时的讲话 (习仲勋) Speech at the Time of Interviewing Representatives of the Fourth Conference of the Daoist Association of China (Xi Zhongxun) (17 Sep 1986)
In 新时期宗教工作文献选编 (Collection of Literature on Religious Work in the New Era) (see below for book details)

贯彻党的宗教政策,团结信教群众为四化建设服务 (习仲勋) Implement the Party's Religion Policy, Unify the Masses of Believers to Build and Serve the Four Modernizations (Xi Zhongxun) (6 Jan 1986)
In 新时期宗教工作文献选编 (Collection of Literature on Religious Work in the New Era) (see below for book details)

一定要抓紧落实党的宗教政策 (习仲勋) We Must Pay Close Attention to Implementing the Party's Religion Policy (Xi Zhongxun) (3 Apr 1985)
In 新时期宗教工作文献选编 (Collection of Literature on Religious Work in the New Era) (see below for book details)

在中国基督教三自爱国运动委员会成立三十周年纪念会上的讲话（杨静仁）Speech Given at the Thirtieth Anniversary Commemoration of the Establishment of the Three-Self Patriotic Movement Committee of the Protestant Churches in China (Yang Jingren) (5 Aug 1984)
In 新时期宗教工作文献选编 (Collection of Literature on Religious Work in the New Era) (see below for book details)

引导宗教界办社会公益事业 (胡乔木) Lead the Religious Circles to Attend to the Cause of Benefiting Society (Hu Qiaomu) (24 Mar 1984)
In 新时期宗教工作文献选编 (Collection of Literature on Religious Work in the New Era) (see below for book details)

宗教信仰自由是我国一项长期的政策 (邓颖超) Freedom of Religious Belief is a Long-term Policy for Our Country (Deng Yingchao) (4 Jun 1983)
In 新时期宗教工作文献选编 (Collection of Literature on Religious Work in the New Era) (see below for book details)

中共中央办公厅，国务院办公厅转发教育部«关于正确处理少数民族地区宗教干扰学校教育问题的意见» CPC Central Office, State Council Office Forwards the Education Department's "Ideas on Properly Dealing with the Problem of Religion Disturbing Education in Minority and Religious Areas" (17 Feb 1983)
In 新时期宗教工作文献选编 (Collection of Literature on Religious Work in the New Era) (see below for book details)

我国公民有宗教信仰的自由 (彭真) Our Citizens Have Freedom of Religious Belief (Pang Zhen) (22 Apr 1982)

In 新时期宗教工作文献选编 (Collection of Literature on Religious Work in the New Era) (see below for book details)

西藏民族解放的道路: 纪念 «关于和平解放西藏办法的协议» 签订三十周年 (李维汉) The Road to Liberating Xizang's Nationalities: Commemorating the Thirtieth Anniversary of the "Agreement Concluding the Manner of Peaceful Liberation of Tibet" (Li Weihan) (23 May 1981)
In 新时期宗教工作文献选编 (Collection of Literature on Religious Work in the New Era) (see below for book details)

一件具有深运意义的盛事 (邓小平) A Thing Holding Far-reaching Significance (Deng Xiaoping) (19 Apr 1980)
In 新时期宗教工作文献选编 (Collection of Literature on Religious Work in the New Era) (see below for book details)

新时期的统一战线和人民政协的任务 (邓小平) Joint Task of the United Front and the People's Government in the New Era (Deng Xiaoping) (15 Jun 1979)
In 新时期宗教工作文献选编 (Collection of Literature on Religious Work in the New Era) (see below for book details)

Party and Government Publications (Internal)

宗教工作的理论与实践: 2003 年全国宗教工作理论务虚会论文集 (Theory and Practice of Religious Work: Collection of Papers from the 2003 National Conference on Religious Work Theory), 宗教文化出版社 (Religion and Culture Press), 2003. 7-80123-532-0/D25
Most recent volume on the latest theory and practice of religious work.

'96 全国省级宗教局长培训班讲座汇编 (Compilation of Lectures from the 1996 Nation-wide Training Meeting for Provincial-level RAB Directors), 1996
This book is a compilation of speeches given at an eleven-day training meeting for provincial-level religious cadres. The training meeting had two purposes: first, to train cadres; second, to analyze religious work under new circumstances—that is, to prevent western infiltration and "peaceful evolution." The training meeting came about as a result of Jiang Zemin's call in June 1996 to raise the quality of cadres, especially the leaders.

Record of the Meeting of the Standing Committee of the Politburo of the Chinese Communist Party Concerning the Maintenance of Stability in Xinjiang (1996)
Discusses how to maintain social stability in Xinjiang Province through closely monitoring the ethnic and religious movements. An English translation is available in Human Rights Watch, *State Control of Religion: Update Number 1* (1999), 9.

理论动态 (*Theoretical Dynamics*)

Theoretical Dynamics is an internal CPC publication issued every ten days. There has been a recent surge in articles about religion: in 2002, no issue featured an article about religion. In the first five months of 2003, three different issues featured a total of seven articles on religion.

齐晓飞 (Qi Xiaofei) 从群众性看宗教的社会历史作用 (Seeing the Role of Religion in Social History from Mass Nature), 理论动态 (*Theoretical Dynamics*), 30 May 2003, 1–7.
This is the first article in the May 2003 issue of 理论动态, an internal CPC Party School publication. The author, Qi Xiaofei, is an assistant director of SARA.

王作安 (Wang Zuo'an), 关于宗教存在长期性的几点思考 (Several Reflections on the Long-Term Nature of Religion), 理论动态 (*Theoretical Dynamics*), 30 May 2003, 8–12.
This is the second article in the May 2003 issue of 理论动态 (Theoretical Dynamics), an internal CPC Party School publication. The author, Wang Zuo'an, is an assistant director of SARA. This is a modified version of an article first published in 中国宗教 (China Religion).

杨同祥 (Yang Tongxiang), 宗教工作者必须把握宗教问题的特殊复杂性 (Religious Workers Must Grasp the Exceptional Complexity of Religious Issues), 理论动态 (*Theoretical Dynamics*), 30 May 2003, 12–14.
This is the third article in the May 2003 issue of 理论动态 (*Theoretical Dynamics*), an internal CPC Party School publication. The author, Yang Tongxiang, is an assistant director of SARA.

杨荣良 (Yang Rongliang), 调动信教群众中的积极因素为全面建设小康社会凝聚力量 (Bring the Positive Factors of the Believing Masses into Play to Embody the Power of All Facets of the Moderately Well-Off Society), 理论动态 (*Theoretical Dynamics*), 30 May 2003, 15–18.
This is the fourth article in the May 2003 issue of 理论动态 (Theoretical Dynamics), an internal CPC Party School publication. The "moderately well-off society" (小康社会) is a phrase introduced by Jiang Zemin. The author, Yang Rongliang, is an inspector for the Nanjing City Nationality and Religious Affairs Bureau.

李爱旻 (Li Aimin), 明确政治定位 维护合法权益 (Clear Political Localization; Safeguard Legal Rights), 理论动态 (*Theoretical Dynamics*), 30 May 2003, 19–21.
This is the fifth article in the May 2003 issue of 理论动态 (Theoretical Dynamics), an internal CPC Party School publication. The author, Li Aimin, is a member of the Hubei Province Nationality and Religious Affairs Committee.

朱瑞志 (Zhu Ruizhi), 积极引导宗教与社会主义社会相适应 (Actively Guide Religion to Adapt Itself to Socialist Society), 理论动态 (*Theoretical Dynamics*), 30 May 2003, 21–24.

This is the sixth article in the May 2003 issue of 理论动态 (Theoretical Dynamics), an internal CPC Party School publication. The author, Zhu Ruizhi, is a member of the Shandong Province Zaozhuang City Nationality and Religious Affairs Bureau.

马宇虹 (Ma Yuhong), 在扩大开放的形式下坚持独立自主自办的原则 (Uphold the Principle of Independent Self-Management under the Situation of Expanded Openness), 理论动态 (*Theoretical Dynamics*), 30 May 2003, 24–28.
This is the final article in the May 2003 issue of 理论动态 (Theoretical Dynamics), an internal CPC Party School publication. The author, Ma Yuhong, is the Director of Business Department #2, the department that supervises Christian activities.

叶小文 (Ye Xiaowen), 对社会主义社会宗教问题的重新认识深刻思考 (A Deep Reflection and a New Understanding of Religious Issues in Socialist Society), 理论动态 (*Theoretical Dynamics*), 20 Jan 2003, 1–12.
This is an important article in the current status of religious work in China. It attempts to synthesize religious policy with Jiang Zemin's "Three Represents" Theory by focusing especially on three of the five "natures" of religion: long-term nature, mass nature, and complex nature.

朱镕基 (Zhu Rongji), 朱镕基总理在考察国家宗教局并接见全国宗教厅局长会议代表时的讲话 (Speech by Premier Zhu Rongji when Inspecting the State Administration for Religious Affairs and Meeting with the Representatives of the Directors of Nationwide Religious Offices), 理论动态 (*Theoretical Dynamics*), 20 Feb 2003 [speech given 10 Jan 2003], 1–7.
The speeches title largely speaks for itself. Then-Premier Zhu Rongji emphasized the religious work of the 16th Party Congress.

Luo Shuze, "Some Hot Issues in Our Work on Religion," 1996.
This internal CCP article details the need to resist foreign infiltration trying to "westernize" and "divide" China, ban cults, enhance cadres' religious education, and strengthen Marxist teachings about atheism. This article was published in the theoretical journal of the CCP, 求是 (*Seeking Truth*), no. 5 (1996), and was translated by Human Rights Watch in *China: State Control of Religion* (see below for book details). Also published in *Chinese Law and Government* 33, no. 2 (Mar/Apr 2000), 101–06.

Party and Government Publications (Public)

Books in Chinese

王作安 (Wang Zuo'an), 中国的宗教问题和宗教政策 (Religious Issues and Religious Policy in China), 宗教文化出版社 (Religion and Culture Press), 2002. 7-80123-442-1
The book is written by Wang Zuo'an, currently the assistant director of SARA. His purpose was to explain the concepts of "religious issues" and "religion policy." The book does a good job of explicating the historical and political factors influencing religion policy. Two of the final chapters, on international religious human rights norms and the influence of globalization, are topics rarely discussed in books on religious policy. The book also reflects the shift in policy after Jiang Zemin's 2001 speech at the religious work conference.

周加才 (Zhou Jiacai), 宗教工作探索 (An Exploration of Religious Work), 宗教文化出版社 (Religion and Culture Press), 2002. 7-80123-387-5
This book was written by the head of the Jiangsu Province RAB, Zhou Jiacai. He writes of his experiences in dealing with religion in Jiangsu Province, as well as essays on theoretical underpinnings, conclusions in dealing with various experiences, and several chapters on Christianity in Hong Kong. The forward was written by Ye Xiaowen, director-general of SARA, giving the book additional legitimacy.

国家宗教事务局政策法规司 编 (edited by SARA's Law and Regulation Department), 全国宗教行政法规规章汇编 (Compilation of National Administrative Rules and Regulations on Religion), 宗教文化出版社 (Religion and Culture Press), 2000. 7-80123-258-5
This is a great compilation of fifty national and provincial regulations related to religion. There is no analysis, only the full texts of the different national and regional regulations.

当代中国丛书编辑委员会 (Contemporary China Editorial Board), 当代中国的宗教工作 (上,下) (Religious Work in Contemporary China, Parts 1 and 2), 当代中国出版社 (Contemporary China Press), 1999. 7-80092-729-6.
This book is part of the "Contemporary China" series, put out in anticipation of the fiftieth anniversary of the founding of the PRC in 1999. The two volumes are a fairly comprehensive survey of the history of religion and religious policy. The reports are largely sanitized and overly positive, but the volumes are very useful for historical comparison. Also has a good section (vol. 1, pages 242–254) on organizations related to religious work. The appendices are also good for research: Appendix is a thorough year-by-year history of government and other events affecting religion from 1949–1995. Appendix 2 contains relevant sections of the major documents affecting religion: the constitution, criminal law, education law, the Basic Laws for Hong Kong and Macau, Decrees 144 & 145, etc. Appendix 3 has the full texts of Document No. 19 (1982) and

Document No. 6 (1991). Appendices 4 and 5 list officials of SARA and patriotic religious associations over time.

中央党校民族宗教理论室编 (Edited by the Central Party School Nationality and Religion Theory Office), 新时期民族宗教工作宣传手册 (Propaganda Handbook on Nationality and Religious Work), 宗教文化出版社 (Religion and Culture Press), 1998. 7-80123-136-8
Meant for Party cadres to better understand Party policies on nationality and religion policy. Its relatively large printing (6000 volumes) indicates that it is a somewhat widely distributed work.

国家宗教事务局政策法规司编 (Edited by SARA's Law & Regulation Department), 宗教工作普法读本 (Religious Work Popular Law Reader), 宗教文化出版社 (Religion and Culture Press), 1997. 7-80123-135-X
This book is recommended by the National Office for Popularizing Law, an effort to make law more accessible to the general public. The book had four printings for a total of 50,000, a huge printing for a religious policy book. The book's main portion is 263 questions and answers. Also included are the standard national laws and regulations that affect religion.

国务院宗教事务局政策规定司 编 (Edited by SARA's Law and Regulation Department), 宗教工作政策要点 (Main Points of Religious Work and Policy), 宗教文化出版社 (Religion and Culture Press), 1996. 7-80123-036-1
This slim volume is a brief summary of China's religious policy, apparently intended for religious cadres and the general public. The printing size (8,000 copies) is relatively large. There is a concluding essay by Ye Xiaowen, currently director-general of SARA. The book doesn't break any new ground, but is a concise, readable, nontheoretical summary of the Party's religion policy.

国务院宗教事务局政策规定司 编 (Edited by SARA's Law and Regulation Department), 宗教政策学习纲要 (Essentials for Studying Religion Policy), 宗教文化出版社 (Religion and Culture Press), 1995. 7-80123-036-1
This book is produced by SARA and directed toward Party cadres. It stresses the need for properly handling the religious question according to law and policy in order to further strengthen the role of the Party and State. This book also warns of the consequences of improper handling of religious issues. One of the assistant editors of the books is Wang Zuo'an, now an assistant director of SARA. The book has a fair amount of analysis as to the undergirding background, philosophy and implementation of China's religion policy.

中共中央献研究室综合研究组，国务院宗教事务局政策法规司 (Edited by CPC Central Committee Research Office Comprehensive Research Group; SARA Law & Policy Department), 新时期宗教工作文献选编 (Collection of Literature on Religious Work in the New Era), 宗教文化出版社 (Religion and Culture Press), 宗教文化出版社 (Religion and Culture Press), 1995. 7-80123-000-0

Collection of sixty-two primary source documents (policies, speeches, regulations, etc.) from 1979–1994, arranged chronologically. There is no analysis. The introduction says that it is directed at Party cadres and research organizations. The short conclusion identifies it as the first publicly published collection of documents related to the Party and government's religious policy.

任一农, 杨牧之, 宋镇铃 主编 (Editors: Ren Yi'nong, Yang Muzhi, Song Zhenling), 民族宗教知识手册 (Handbook on Nationalities and Religion), 中共中央党校出版社 (CPC Central Party School Press), 1994. 7-5035-0940-6
This book was published as part of a series on "News, Publishing, and Culture Propaganda Workers Must Be Prepared" (新闻,出版, 文化宣传工作者必备). It was intended to help these types of workers resolve error and give correct answers to questions related to nationalities and religion. It is a nice source for primary source documents, especially speeches and policy documents, and nice for finding concise answers to questions (chapter 5). The book also has contact information for regional RAB and nationality bureaus in Appendix 3. The book is a bit dated (1994).

龚学增，靳薇 胡岩 编著 (Authors/Editors: Gong Xuezeng, Jin Wei, Hu Yan), 民族问题与宗教问题讲座 (Lectures on Nationality and Religious Issues), 中共中央党校出版社 (CPC Central Party School Press), 1994. 7-5035-1064-1
This book was written by several lecturers at the Central Party School: they edited their lectures on nationality and religion policy and put out this book. The subject matter was the topic for a course taught there.

国务院宗教事务局编 (Edited by SARA), 宗教工作基础知识 (Basic Knowledge about Religious Work), 中国旅游出版社 (China Tourism Press), 1990. 7-5032-0343-9
This book is intended for religious cadres to assist them in studying and researching religious issues. The chief editor is Wang Zuo'an, now assistant director of SARA. The 7,500-volume printing indicates that it was fairly widely distributed. The book has detailed descriptions of the government's view—historical and contemporary—of the traditional religions as well as details about religions associated with thirty-two of the country's nationalities. The book also has long sections on religion in Hong Kong, Macau, and Taiwan. The appendix has three pages of references to other social science works dealing with religion.

中国社会科学院民族研究所民族理论室 (Chinese Academy of Social Sciences, Nationality Research Center, Nationality Theory Office), 宗教与民族研究资料选辑 (Compilation of Selected Research and Information on Religion and Nationalities), 中国社会科学院民族研究所民族理论室 (Chinese Academy of Social Sciences, Nationality Research Center, Nationality Theory Office), 1986. No ISBN
This book is a collection of essays written by Chinese social scientists about religion, nationality, and the relationship between the two. The book is a bit dated (1986), but still contains some interesting insights from the social science perspectives on the relationship between nationality and religion.

Periodical Articles in Chinese

中国宗教 *China Religion*

China Religion is a public-circulation monthly magazine for people in religious circles and religious cadres. It features articles written by SARA officials and other religious cadres, as well as highlights of (officially-sanctioned) religious activities.

秋石(Qiu Shi) [叶小文 Ye Xiaowen], 社会主义的宗教论 (Socialism's View of Religion), in 中国宗教 (*China Religion*), May 2003, 6–10.
This article was ghostwritten by SARA Director-General Ye Xiaowen. He shows how Jiang Zemin's "Three Represents" Theory fits with the Party's religious policy. This article originally appeared in a 2003 issue of 求是 (*Seeking Truth*), a Party magazine.

叶小文 (Ye Xiaowen), 为什么要钻研 "社会主义的宗教论" (Why We Must Carefully Study "Socialism's View of Religion"), 中国宗教(*China Religion*), May 2003, 12–16.
This article is a supplement to the one immediately before it, "Socialism's View of Religion." Both are written by Ye Xiaowen, the director-general of SARA. This article is a question and answer session with the author (the same person), an attempt to better explain the principles.

杨同祥 (Yang Tongxiang), 宗教工作者必须把握宗教问题的特殊复杂性 (Religious Workers Must Grasp the Exceptionally Complex Nature of Religion), 中国宗教 (*China Religion*), Apr 2003, 11–12.
This is an article written in *China Religion,* a public-circulation magazine for people in religious circles and religious cadres. The title is fairly self-explanatory.

叶小文 (Ye Xiaowen), 崇尚和谐 服务社会 (Uphold Harmony, Serve Society), 中国宗教 (*China Religion*), Apr 2003, 10.
This is a speech given by Ye Xiaowen, the director-general of SARA, at a commemoration of Laozi's birth. The speech is featured in *China Religion,* a public-circulation magazine for people in religious circles and religious cadres.

叶小文 (Ye Xiaowen), 对美国西部基督教领袖的演讲 (Address Delivered to Christian Leaders in the West of the United States), 中国宗教 (*China Religion*), Mar 2003 (pages 50-52), Apr 2003, 41–43 [speech given 27 Feb 2003].
The director-general of SARA, Ye Xiaowen, delivered this speech in Los Angeles. The speech was reprinted, with side-by-side English translation, in the March and April 2003 issues of 中国宗教 (*China Religion*).

王作安 (Wang Zuo'an), 关于宗教存在长期性的几点思考 (Several Reflections on the Long-Term Existence of Religion), 中国宗教 (*China Religion*), Feb 2003, 9–11.

This is an article written by Wang Zuo'an, the assistant director of SARA. The article was slightly modified and reprinted in a 30 May 2003 issue of 理论动态 (Theoretical Dynamics).

«人民日报» 记者郑宏范 (*People's Daily* writer Zheng Hongfan), 朱镕基在国家宗教事务局考察工作 (Zhu Rongji Inspecting the State Administration for Religious Affairs), 中国宗教 (*China Religion*), Jan 2003, 4–5.
This is a reprint of a *People's Daily* article reporting on Premier Zhu Rongji's address to religious work cadres. He emphasized implementing the "spirit of the 16th Party Congress" and the importance of doing a good job of religious work.

叶小文 (Ye Xiaowen), 对社会主义社会宗教问题的思考 (Another Reflection on the Question of Religion and Socialist Society), 中国宗教 (*China Religion*), Jan 2003, 9–13.
The author of this article is Ye Xiaowen, the director-general of SARA. He points out among other things, that religion has a deep history in society and will continue to exist for a long time, that religion is wrapped up in economics, politics, and cultural issues, that religion has an important influence on the development and stability of society, and that religion is an important factor in international relations and politics. Further, the principle of independence and self-management must prevent religion from being used by "enemies" within and without the nation seeking opportunities to infiltrate.

Public Security-related Documents, Manuals, and Publications (Internal)

These documents are publicly available on Web sites and in university libraries. The documents and their content cannot be verified for authenticity and should be used with discretion.

公安部一局 编 (Edited by the Ministry of Public Security Bureau 1), 反动会道门简介 (Introduction to Reactionary Secret Societies), 群众出版社 (Mass Press), 1985.
Describes the government's collected information on secret societies and all their permutations. A bit dated (1985), but this book (intended for internal use) shows how the Ministry of Public Security manages religious groups. The book includes ways of identifying the different organizations, as well as organizational charts.

*The documents listed immediately below are from the Web site of the Committee for Investigation of Persecution of Religion in China (中国宗教迫害真相调查委员会) (http://www.china21.org). Chinese authorities have not officially acknowledged the existence of these documents.

保定市公安局 关于印发«对天主教工作对象开展基础调查的实施方案» 的通知 (Baoding City Public Security Bureau: Notice about the Distribution of the Workplan on Implementing the Launch of a Basic Investigation into Catholic Work Objectives), 20 Jun 2002
This is an internal document from the Public Security Bureau of Baoding City in Hebei Province. It details an investigation into the work of the Catholic Church (both "official" and "underground"). See also the Baoding Public Security Documents of 15 Jul 2002 and 22 Aug 2002.

保定市公安局宗教处关于做好我市在境外神职人员调查工作的通知 (Notice of the Baoding City Public Security Bureau Religion Section: Complete the Investigative Work into the Foreign Clergy in Our City), 15 Jul 2002
This is an internal document from the Public Security Bureau of Baoding City in Hebei Province. It details an investigation into the work of the Catholic Church (both "official" and "underground"). In particular, the investigation calls for determining information about clergy: their identities (name, foreign name, address, etc.), backgrounds, records of comings and goings from China, relations, work records, criminal records, activities, etc.

保定市公安局: 关于印发«制止基督教非法活动的工作方案» 的通知 (Baoding City Public Security Bureau: Notice about the Distribution of the Work Plan on Terminating Illegal Christian Activities), 22 Aug 2002
This is an internal document from the Public Security Bureau of Baoding City in Hebei Province. It details a crackdown on "illegal" Christian activities (i.e., unregistered and

"cult" organizations). See also the Baoding Public Security Documents of 20 Jun 2002 and 15 Jul 2002. Printed from Persecution.com.

北京市公安局国内安全保卫总队文件: 关于邪教组织 "华南教会" 活动情况的通报 (Beijing Public Security Bureau Internal Safety and Safeguards Team Document: Circular on the Activities of the Cult Organization "South China Christianity"), 9 Aug 2001
This internal public security memo is a description of the crackdown in Beijing on the "South China Christianity" organization, labeled a cult by the government. An appendix details ten leaders of the organization. At
www.china21.org/simpChinese/docs/sim_7th.htm. The document was translated into English as part of Freedom House's "Seven Secret Documents" publication.

安徽省公安厅办公室: 明确任务坚定信心努力开创新世纪国内安全保卫工作的新局面 (Anhui Province Public Security Office: Unequivocally Try Hard with Confidence and Steadfastness in the Assignment to Create a New Situation in the Work of Internal Safety and Safeguards in the New Century), 6 Mar 2001
This memo is a speech given at a provincial security work conference in 2001. It discusses the work that went on in 2000 and the plan for 2001 and the future of dealing with "cult" organizations (including Falungong) and other "enemies" in the province. The memo was sent to public security bureaus around the province, as well as a copy to the provincial Party Public Security committee and the national Ministry of Public Security. At www.china21.org/simpChinese/docs/sim_3rd.htm. The document was translated into English as part of Freedom House's "Seven Secret Documents" publication.

吉林省公安厅, 吉林省高级人民法院: 关于严厉打击非法组织的通知 (Jilin Province Public Security Office, Jilin Province High People's Court: Notice of Severe Attack on Illegal Organizations), 20 May 2000
This internal public security memo was written "in preparation for the 2008 Olympics" to crackdown on illegal organizations. Meetings of three or more peoples may be detained for up to 15 days and fined 1000 *yuan*. For wide-scale meetings, activities, speeches, and for those unwilling to change, they can be imprisoned for up to 3 years and fined 10,000 *yuan*. For organizers of illegal organizations, they can be arrested, punished severely immediately. For Falungong practitioners, the severity of attack must be increased: as soon as they are discovered, they can be arrested. The regulations are to be in place from 20 May 2000 to 30 Dec 2007. At
http://www.china21.org/simpChinese/docs/0501_document_jilin.htm.

黑龙江省公安厅: 业务工作大事记 (Heilongjiang Province Public Security Office: Record of Major Work Events), 4 Sep 2000
This is an internal public security memo giving a day-by-day description of provincial public security leaders and their actions in the "attack the cults" (打邪) crackdown on Falungong and other "cults" in August 2000. At http://www.china21.org/docs/CONFI-HEILONHJIANG-CHINESE.htm. The document was translated into English as part of Freedom House's "Seven Secret Documents" publication.

河北省公安厅宗教处毕荣生副处长在"807"邪教组织"实际神"专案协调会上的讲话 (Speech by Hebei Province Public Security Office Religion Section Assistant Director Bi Rongsheng at the "August 7" Special Task Force on the "Real God" Cult Organization), 14 Sep 2000
This is a speech given by a Public Security official detailing the crackdown on the Real God Church, an organization labeled a cult by the government. At http://www.china21.org/simpChinese/docs/shijiazhuang/index.htm. The document was translated into English as part of Freedom House's "Seven Secret Documents" publication.

中华人民共和国公安部关于认定和取缔邪教组织若干问题的通知: 现已认定的邪教组织情况 (PRC Ministry of Public Security Notice: Certain Questions on Resolving and Banning Cult Organizations: Already Banned Cult Organizations), 30 Apr 2000.
This internal public security memo was crafted and sent to many bureaus. It details the background and situation on several banned organizations: the Shouters, Society of Disciples, Full-Scope Church, Spirit Church, New Testament Church, Guanyin Famen, Lord God Church, Established King Church, Unification Church, Three Kinds of Servants Sect, "Spirit Immortal Real Buddha Religion," Heavenly Father's Children, Dami Mission, and Elijah Sect. At http://www.china21.org/simpChinese/docs/sim_1st.htm. The document was translated into English as part of Freedom House's "Seven Secret Documents" publication.

安徽省公安厅关于进一步加强对邪教组织"全能神"侦查工作的通知 (Anhui Province Public Security Office Notice on Improving and Strengthening the Investigative Work toward the "Almighty God" Cult Organization), 2 Apr 1999
This internal Public Security memo details the investigation and crackdown on the "Almighty God" organization, labeled as a cult by the government. At http://www.china21.org/docs/CONFI-ANHUI-1-CHINESE.htm. The document was translated into English as part of Freedom House's "Seven Secret Documents" publication.

Secondary Sources

Listed below are other secondary sources, publications, and books related to religious freedom in China that are not easily classified above, listed in reverse chronological order. Rather than select a particular citation style, the following patterns are used:

Books: Author (translation), *Title* (translation), (publisher (translation), date). ISBN

Journal articles: Author (translation), "Article Title," *Journal Name* volume (date), pages. ISSN

Books and Periodical Articles in English

Jason Kindopp and Carol Lee Hamrin, eds., *God and Caesar in China: Policy Implications of Church-State Tensions* (Brookings Institution Press, 2004). 0-8157-4936-8
This book is a collection of essays on religious policy in China, the growth of Christian faiths in China, and the impact of church-state tensions on China's international relations. Essays include Jason Kindopp, "Policy Dilemmas in China's Church-State Relations: An Introduction"; Daniel H. Bays, "A Tradition of State Dominance"; Mickey Spiegel, "Control and Containment in the Reform Era"; Kim-Kwong Chan, "Accession to the World Trade Organization and State Adaptation"; Jean-Paul Wiest, "Setting Roots: The Catholic Church in China to 1949"; Richard Madsen, "Catholic Conflict and Cooperation in the People's Republic of China"; Yihua Xu, "'Patriotic' Protestants: The Making of an Official Church"; Jason Kindopp, "Fragmented yet Defiant: Protestant Resilience under Chinese Communist Party Rule"; Peng Liu, "Unreconciled Differences: The Staying Power of Religion"; Carol Lee Hamrin, "Advancing Religious Freedom in a Global China: Conclusions."

Kim-Kwong Chan, "China's Socioeconomic Changes and the Implications for the Religion-State Dynamic in China," *BYU Law Review* (summer 2004): 325–56. ISSN 0360-151X
This recent article analyzes the impact China's WTO accession may have on religious freedom in China.

Ronald C. Keith and Zhiqiu Lin, "The '*Falun Gong* Problem': Politics and the Struggle for the Rule of Law in China," *The China Quarterly* 175 (September 2003), 623–42. ISSN: 0305-7410
This recent article argues that the politicization of law (particularly the criminal law's emphasis on counter-revolution) in dealing with Falungong threatens progress toward the rule of law in China.

Pitman B. Potter, "Belief in Control: Regulation of Religion in China," *The China Quarterly* 174 (June 2003), 317–37. ISSN: 0305-7410

An excellent contemporary view of China's religion policy from the perspective of patterns of compliance and resistance, concluding that China's efforts to control religion could challenge the regime's legitimacy.

Daniel C.K. Chow, *The Legal System of the People's Republic of China in a Nutshell* (West Law School, 2003). 0-3142-6297-0
This book is a recent and very readable introduction to China's rather confusing legal system, recommended for the legal and non-legal scholar alike. Despite its "Nutshell" title, the book is nearly 500 pages, though most of the information is valuable. The author, Daniel Chow, is a law professor at Ohio State University who has spent a great deal of time in China.

Dui Hua Foundation (中美对话), *Selection of Cases from the Criminal Law: Banned Protestant Groups* (刑事案件选编: 被取缔新教组织), 2003. No ISBN
Compiled by an American human rights organization, the Dui Hua Foundation, this book is a collection of criminal law cases taken from articles in regional newspapers. The editors have translated the Chinese text in full and prepared a helpful introduction. The cases deal with 14 banned sects, and the publication gives specific details on each sect's background and current status in China.

Human Rights Watch, *Dangerous Meditation: China's Campaign against Falungong* (Human Rights Watch, 2002). 1-56432-270-X
This book is a concise (117 pages) overview of the crackdown on Falungong, including translations and excerpts of relevant government documents. Partial translations include "Social Organizations Regulations," "The Assembly Law and Implementing Regulations," "Public Order Regulations," "The PRC Criminal Law," "State Secrets and State Security Laws," "Law Governing Electronic and Print Media," and "Internet Regulations."

Betty L. Wong, "A Paper Tiger? An Examination of the International Religious Freedom Act's Impact on Christianity in China," 24 *Hastings International & Comparative Law Review*, 539–60. ISSN: 0149-9246
A legal look at the (in)effectiveness of the U.S.' International Religious Freedom Act in curbing religious persecution in China. The author concludes that educational exchange programs are more effective than direct political pressure.

Tibet Information Network, *Relative Freedom?: Tibetan Buddhism and Religious Policy in Kandze, Sichuan, 1987–1999* (Tibet Information Network (西藏信息網) 1999). ISSN 1355-5650
This book has a very narrow focus—one prefecture in Sichuan. It contains translations of government documents and detailed descriptions of human rights abuses in the prefecture.

Darin W. Carlson, "Understanding Chinese–U.S. Conflict over Freedom of Religion: The Wolf-Specter Freedom from Religious Persecution Acts of 1997 and 1998," 1998 *BYU Law Review* (1998), 563–606.

While this U.S. law review article is based solely on English-language sources, it gives a fairly accurate overview of the situation and the potential for religious freedom to be a large stumbling block in U.S.–China relations, as well as explaining why China has not reacted to U.S. and international pressure to relax control over religion.

Human Rights Watch Asia, *China: State Control of Religion* (Human Rights Watch, 1997). 1-56432-224-6
While slightly dated, the book contains several useful translations of important documents: "Some Hot Issues in Our Work on Religion," "Document of the Office of the Tongxiang Municipal Committee of the Chinese Communist Party," "Document of the Donglai Township Committee of the Chinese Communist Party," "Regulations from the Shanghai Religious Affairs Bureau," "Excerpts from Questions and Answers on the Patriotic Education Program in Monasteries," "Regulations on the Supervision of the Religious Activities of Foreigners in China," "Regulations Regarding the Management of Places of Religious Activities," "Registration Procedures for Venues of Religious Activities," "Method for the Annual Inspection of Places of Religious Activities," and "Chinese Current Religious Question: Once Again an Inquiry into the Five Characteristics of Religion." The book's contents are also online at http://www.hrw.org/reports/1997/china1.

Donald E. MacInnis, "From Suppression to Repression: Religion in China Today," *Current History*, Sept. 1996, 284–89. ISSN: 0011-3530
This article gives a brief but nuanced overview of religious policy in China.

Tibet Information Network and Human Rights Watch, Cutting Off the Serpent's Head: Tightening Control in Tibet, 1994–1995, Human Rights Watch, 1996. 1-56432-166-5
This book is specific to Tibet, but its appendices contain translations of documents from the Tibet government.

R. Lanier Britsch, "The Current Legal Status of Christianity in China," 1995 *BYU Law Review* (1995), 345–99. ISSN: 0360-151X
While this U.S. law review article based only on English-language sources, it is a concise background document on legal issues related to religious freedom. The author gives prescient insight on the legal challenges facing Christianity in China. Four appendices give the full-translated texts of Document No. 19, Document No. 6, Decree 144, and Decree 145. Some of the information is slightly out of date.

Beatrice Leung, "Religious Freedom and the Constitution in the People's Republic of China: Interpretation and Implementation," *DISKUS* 3:1 (1995), 1–18.
Written by a Hong Kong scholar, this is an accurate (if slightly outdated) history of religious policy in China. The article can also be found at http://www.uni-marburg.de/religionswissenschaft/journal/diskus/leung.html.

Chan Kim-Kwong and Alan Hunter, "New Light on Religious Policy in the PRC," *Issues and Studies* 31 (Feb 1995), 21–36. ISSN 1013-2511

This brief study gives an overview of China's religious policy, focusing on the late 1980s and early 1990s. The piece also includes English translations of six secret central documents from 1988 to 1991 that related to religious affairs.

Chan Kim-Kwong and Alan Hunter, "Religion and Society in Mainland China in the 1990s," *Issues and Studies* 30 (Aug 1994), 52–68. ISSN 1013-2511
The study gives a historical and sociological profile of religion in twentieth-century China.

Eric Kolodner, Comment, "Religious Rights in China: A Comparison of International Human Rights Law and Chinese Domestic Legislation," 12 *UCLA Pacific Basin Law Journal*, summer 1994, 407–30. ISSN 0884-0768
This is a great piece that details the status of China's compliance (or lack thereof) with international treaties and norms. It's a bit dated but lays a good foundation for future work.

Human Rights in China, "Human Rights in China 1993," *China Rights Forum*, spring 1994, 20.

Human Rights Watch, *Continuing Religious Repression in China* (Human Rights Watch, 1993). 1-56432-102-9

Asia Watch (Human Rights Watch), *Freedom of Religion in China* (Human Rights Watch, 1992). 1-56432-050-2
This slim volume (79 pages) is a brief overview of freedom of religion in China. The appendices translate several important government documents in full.

Chan Kim-Kwong, "A Chinese Perspective on the Interpretation of the Chinese Government's Religious Policy," in *All under Heaven: Chinese Tradition and Christian Life in the People's Republic of China* (Alan Hunter and Don Rimmington, eds.), 1992, 38.

Luo Zhufeng, ed. *Religion under Socialism in China* (Donald E. MacInnis & Zheng Xi'an trans; M.E. Sharpe, 1991). 0-87332-609-1
Though a bit dated, this book is a good theoretical and philosophical overview of the government's position toward religion. The first half of the book traces the China's religious policy through history; the second half is a collection of case studies written by field work about specific religious group.

Donald E. MacInnis, *Religion in China Today: Policy and Practice* (Orbis, 1989). 0-88344-645-6
This thick book is a compendium of various regulations and publications, translated into English that affect religion in China. It's a bit dated, but remains a good backgrounder for grasping the nuances of religion in China.

Philip L. Wickeri, *Seeking the Common Ground: Protestant Christianity, the Three-Self Movement, and China's United Front* (1988).

China News and Church Report (CNCR)
Published by the Chinese Church Research Center in Taiwan, this monthly/bimonthly publication publishes update on the status of Protestant Churches in China. Several of the issues also feature translated regulations.

Books and Periodical Articles in Chinese

行政院大陆委员会 编印 (Administrative Academy Mainland Committee), 大陆地区宗教法规彙编 (Edited Religious Regulations of the Mainland), 行政院大陆委员会 编印 (Administrative Academy Mainland Committee), 1995. 957-00-5660-6
This book is a collection of primary source documents (in traditional characters, because the book is from Taiwan). While most of the documents can be found elsewhere, this is one of the few books that breaks down the regulations topically rather than chronologically. Section 2 contains the constitutions of the national religious associations. The 1995 date means that some of these regulations have been superseded, but the documents are useful to see how regulations have changed over time. The "other" section (Chapter 9) has some interesting oddball regulations. Confusingly, each section has its own page numbering.

红色牧师：董健吾 (Red Pastor: Dong Jianwu) (2000).
Biography of Dong Jianwu (1891–1970) who was an ordained minister of the Anglican Church and a secret Communist Party member during the 1920s and 1930s. Not as useful for policy studies, but an interesting story nonetheless.

中共问题原始资料编辑委员会 (Problems of the CPC Firsthand Information Editorial Board), 中共怎样对待宗教: 原始资料彙编之八（上和下）(How the CPC Deals with Religion: A Collection of Eight First-hand Essays (Parts 1 and 2)), 黎明文化事业股份有限公司 (Li Ming Cultural Enterprises) (1984). No ISBN
This book from Taiwan (traditional characters) has a very negative view of the CPC and its policy on religion. It reads more like a human rights organization exposé than a true scholarly work. Its 1984 publication makes it a bit out of date, but many of the charges leveled by the book still have merit. The book also contains many rather obscure primary source documents from the Mao and early Deng eras.

Internet Sources

In addition to the Web sites mentioned above, several other Web sites in China and in the West contain valuable, primary and secondary source materials on regulations that affect religion in China. These are grouped by language and source.

Internet Sources in English

GOVERNMENT WEB SITES
U.S. State Department International Religious Freedom Report on China (http://www.state.gov/g/drl/rls/irf/2004/35396pf.htm)
The U.S. State Department's Annual Report is a fairly thorough summary of the status of religious freedom in each country. Past reports can be found at http://www.state.gov/g/drl/rls/irf.

U.S. Commission on International Religious Freedom (http://www.uscirf.gov)
Established in 1998, the Commission monitors religious freedom in other countries and advises the President, Secretary of State, and Congress on how to best promote religious freedom worldwide. It publishes reports similar to the U.S. State Department; CIRF reports on fewer countries but makes policy recommendations.
http://www.uscirf.gov/reports/12May04/finalReport.php3#_china.

Congressional-Executive Commission on China (http://www.cecc.gov)
The commission was created by Congress in 2000 to prepare an annual report on the development of human rights and the rule of law in China. The Web site also has many of the religious freedom laws in Chinese and English. The 2004 report is available at http://www.cecc.gov/pages/annualRpt/annualRpt04/CECCannRpt2004.pdf.

HUMAN RIGHTS ORGANIZATIONS
Amnesty International (http://web.amnesty.org/library/eng-chn/index)
Though Amnesty reports definitely have a strong opinion, they are accurate and concise reports about human rights violations in a specific part of the world (and country, sometimes).

Committee for Investigation on Persecution of Religion in China (http://www.china21.org/English/index.htm)
Like Amnesty, the reports tend to be one-sided but very accurate and prescient. Many of the articles do not have sources. The documents listed at the bottom of the Chinese section are top secret public security documents. See also the Chinese site (detailed below)

Freedom House Center for Religious Freedom (http://www.freedomhouse.org/religion/)
Freedom House is a U.S.-based human rights group. Its Center for Religious Freedom division conducts investigative reports and publishes books and studies. The Center also published "Report Analyzing Seven Secret Chinese Government Documents" in 2002.

Human Rights Watch (http://www.hrw.org/asia/china.php)
Like Amnesty International, Human Rights Watch seeks to publicize human rights abuses around the world. They have an extensive listing of publications on China (http://docsmgmt.hrw.org/china-pubs.php). Some documents are posted on HRW but are difficult to find.

International Coalition for Religious Freedom
(www.religiousfreedom.com/wrpt/Chinarpt.htm)
Prepares annual reports similar to the U.S. State Department on the condition of religious freedom around the world. The latest report on China is May 2002.

OTHER
China's Human Rights (http://www.humanrights-china.org)
This Web site is sponsored either directly or indirectly by the government, and seeks to portray China's human rights record in the most positive light. It is a good reference point for titles and dates of regulations in English.

Religion and Law Research Consortium (http://www.religlaw.org)
Sponsored by an association of U.S. and Western European church-state scholars, this Web site hosts a searchable database of constitution, laws, and regulations from around the world that affect religion. The Web site is in the ongoing process of posting nearly 200 regulations and other religion-related documents from China in Chinese and English.

Internet Sources in Chinese

GOVERNMENT SITES
中共中央统一战线工作部: 政策与法规 (*United Front*)
(http://www.zytzb.org.cn/zytzbwz/flfg/)
The United Front Web site's section on religious laws lists about 55 national- and provincial-level regulations related to religion.

人民网法律在线 (*People's Daily Web Online Law*)
(http://law.people.com.cn/bike/index.btml)
The law Web site of the People's Daily law Web site has daily updates. Since the media is state-run, the information is (presumably) accurate. Searchable, but no links to the actual regulations. Links to other legal sites.

司法部 (*Ministry of Justice*) (http://www.legalinfo.gov.cn/)
Web site hosted by China's Ministry of Justice. Searchable, though the results are not always comprehensive.

HUMAN RIGHTS ORGANIZATIONS

中国宗教迫害真相调查委员会 (*Committee for Investigation on Persecution of Religion in China*) (http://www.china21.org)

The reports tend to be one-sided but very accurate and prescient. Many of the articles do not have sources. The documents listed at the bottom of the site are top secret public security documents. See also the English site (detailed above).

OTHER

信德: 政策法规 (*Faith Web site: Policy and Regulations*)
(http://chinacatholic.org/LAW/LAW.HTM)

The Web site of the (officially recognized) China Catholic Church has several laws and policy papers, particularly ones affecting Catholics.

Religion and Law Research Consortium (http://religlaw.org)

Sponsored by an association of U.S. and Western European church-state scholars, this Web site hosts a searchable database of constitution, laws, and regulations from around the world that affect religion. The Web site is in the ongoing process of posting nearly 200 regulations and other religion-related documents from China in Chinese and English.

APPENDIX:
RELIGIOUS AFFAIRS REGULATIONS

国务院公布《宗教事务条例》

明年３月施行（全文）

中华人民共和国国务院令（第４２６号）

中华人民共和国国务院令

第４２６号

《宗教事务条例》已经２００４年７月７日国务院第５７次常务会议通过，现予公布，自２００５年３月１日起施行。

总 理 温家宝

二００四年十一月三十日

宗教事务条例

第一章 总 则

第一条 为了保障公民宗教信仰自由，维护宗教和睦与社会和谐，规范宗教事务管理，根据宪法和有关法律，制定本条例。

第二条 公民有宗教信仰自由。

任何组织或者个人不得强制公民信仰宗教或者不信仰宗教，不得歧视信仰宗教的公民（以下称信教公民）或者不信仰宗教的公民（以下称不信教公民）。

信教公民和不信教公民、信仰不同宗教的公民应当相互尊重、和睦相处。

第三条 国家依法保护正常的宗教活动，维护宗教团体、宗教活动场所和信教公民的合法权益。

宗教团体、宗教活动场所和信教公民应当遵守宪法、法律、法规和规章，维护国家统一、民族团结和社会稳定。

任何组织或者个人不得利用宗教进行破坏社会秩序、损害公民身体健康、妨碍国家教育制度，以及其他损害国家利益、社会公共利益和公民合法权益的活动。

第四条 各宗教坚持独立自主自办的原则，宗教团体、宗教活动场所和宗教事务不受外国势力的支配。

宗教团体、宗教活动场所、宗教教职人员在友好、平等的基础上开展对外交往；其他组织或者个人在对外经济、文化等合作、交流活动中不得接受附加的宗教条件。

第五条 县级以上人民政府宗教事务部门依法对涉及国家利益和社会公共利益的宗教事务进行行政管理，县级以上人民政府其他有关部门在各自职责范围内依法负责有关的行政管理工作。

各级人民政府应当听取宗教团体、宗教活动场所和信教公民的意见，协调宗教事务管理工作。

第二章 宗教团体

第六条 宗教团体的成立、变更和注销，应当依照《社会团体登记管理条例》的规定办理登记。

宗教团体章程应当符合《社会团体登记管理条例》的有关规定。

宗教团体按照章程开展活动，受法律保护。

第七条 宗教团体按照国家有关规定可以编印宗教内部资料性出版物。出版公开发行的宗教出版物，按照国家出版管理的规定办理。

涉及宗教内容的出版物，应当符合《出版管理条例》的规定，并不得含有下列内容：

（一）破坏信教公民与不信教公民和睦相处的；

（二）破坏不同宗教之间和睦以及宗教内部和睦的；

（三）歧视、侮辱信教公民或者不信教公民的；

（四）宣扬宗教极端主义的；

（五）违背宗教的独立自主自办原则的。

第八条 设立宗教院校，应当由全国性宗教团体向国务院宗教事务部门提出申请，或者由省、自治区、直辖市宗教团体向拟设立的宗教院校所在地的省、自治区、直辖市人民政府宗教事务部门提出申请。省、自治区、直辖市人民政府宗教事务部门应当自收到申请之日起３０日内提出意见，对拟同意的，报国务院宗教事务部门审批。

国务院宗教事务部门应当自收到全国性宗教团体的申请或者省、自治区、直辖市人民政府宗教事务部门设立宗教院校的报告之日起６０日内，作出批准或者不予批准的决定。

第九条 设立宗教院校，应当具备下列条件：

（一）有明确的培养目标、办学章程和课程设置计划；

（二）有符合培养条件的生源；

（三）有必要的办学资金和稳定的经费来源；

（四）有教学任务和办学规模所必需的教学场所、设施设备；

（五）有专职的院校负责人、合格的专职教师和内部管理组织；

（六）布局合理。

第十条 全国性宗教团体可以根据本宗教的需要按照规定选派和接收宗教留学人员。

第十一条 信仰伊斯兰教的中国公民前往国外朝觐，由伊斯兰教全国性宗教团体负责组织。

第三章 宗教活动场所

第十二条 信教公民的集体宗教活动，一般应当在经登记的宗教活动场所（寺院、宫观、清真寺、教堂以及其他固定宗教活动处所）内举行，由宗教活动场所或者宗教团体组织，由宗教教职人员或者符合本宗教规定的其他人员主持，按照教义教规进行。

第十三条 筹备设立宗教活动场所，由宗教团体向拟设立的宗教活动场所所在地的县级人民政府宗教事务部门提出申请。县级人民政府宗教事务部门应当自收到申请之日起３０日内，对拟同意的，报设区的市级人民政府宗教事务部门审批。

设区的市级人民政府宗教事务部门应当自收到县级人民政府宗教事务部门的报告之日起３０日内，对拟同意设立寺院、宫观、清真寺、教堂的，提出审核意见，报省、自治区、直辖市人民政府宗教事务部门审批；对设立其他固定宗教活动处所的，作出批准或者不予批准的决定。

省、自治区、直辖市人民政府宗教事务部门应当自收到设区的市级人民政府宗教事务部门拟同意设立寺院、宫观、清真寺、教堂的报告之日起３０日内，作出批准或者不予批准的决定。

宗教团体在宗教活动场所的设立申请获批准后，方可办理该宗教活动场所的筹建事项。

第十四条 设立宗教活动场所，应当具备下列条件：

（一）设立宗旨不违背本条例第三条、第四条的规定；

（二）当地信教公民有经常进行集体宗教活动的需要；

（三）有拟主持宗教活动的宗教教职人员或者符合本宗教规定的其他人员；

（四）有必要的资金；

（五）布局合理，不妨碍周围单位和居民的正常生产、生活。

第十五条 宗教活动场所经批准筹备并建设完工后，应当向所在地的县级人民政府宗教事务部门申请登记。县级人民政府宗教事务部门应当自收到申请之日起３０日内对该宗教活动场所的管理组织、规章制度建设等情况进行审核，对符合条件的予以登记，发给《宗教活动场所登记证》。

第十六条 宗教活动场所合并、分立、终止或者变更登记内容的，应当到原登记管理机关办理相应的变更登记手续。

第十七条 宗教活动场所应当成立管理组织，实行民主管理。宗教活动场所管理组织的成员，经民主协商推选，并报该场所的登记管理机关备案。

第十八条 宗教活动场所应当加强内部管理，依照有关法律、法规、规章的规定，建立健全人员、财务、会计、治安、消防、文物保护、卫生防疫等管理制度，接受当地人民政府有关部门的指导、监督、检查。

第十九条 宗教事务部门应当对宗教活动场所遵守法律、法规、规章情况，建立和执行场所管理制度情况，登记项目变更情况，以及宗教活动和涉外活动情况进行监督检查。宗教活动场所应当接受宗教事务部门的监督检查。

第二十条 宗教活动场所可以按照宗教习惯接受公民的捐献，但不得强迫或者摊派。

非宗教团体、非宗教活动场所不得组织、举行宗教活动，不得接受宗教性的捐献。

第二十一条 宗教活动场所内可以经销宗教用品、宗教艺术品和宗教出版物。

经登记为宗教活动场所的寺院、宫观、清真寺、教堂（以下称寺观教堂）按照国家有关规定可以编印宗教内部资料性出版物。

第二十二条 跨省、自治区、直辖市举行超过宗教活动场所容纳规模的大型宗教活动，或者在宗教活动场所外举行大型宗教活动，应当由主办的宗教团体、寺观教堂在拟举行日的３０日前，向大型宗教活动举办地的省、自治区、直辖市人民政府宗教事务部门提出申请。省、自治区、直辖市人民政府宗教事务部门应当自收到申请之日起１５日内作出批准或者不予批准的决定。

大型宗教活动应当按照批准通知书载明的要求依宗教仪轨进行，不得违反本条例第三条、第四条的有关规定。主办的宗教团体、寺观教堂应当采取有效措施防止意外事故的发生。大型宗教活动举办地的乡、镇人民政府和县级以上地方人民政府有关部门应当依据各自职责实施必要的管理，保证大型宗教活动安全、有序进行。

第二十三条 宗教活动场所应当防范本场所内发生重大事故或者发生违犯宗教禁忌等伤害信教公民宗教感情、破坏民族团结、影响社会稳定的事件。

发生前款所列事故或者事件时，宗教活动场所应当立即报告所在地的县级人民政府宗教事务部门。

第二十四条 宗教团体、寺观教堂拟在宗教活动场所外修建大型露天宗教造像，应当由省、自治区、直辖市宗教团体向省、自治区、直辖市人民政府宗教事务部门提出申请。省、自治区、直辖市人民政府宗教事务部门应当自收到申请之日起３０日内提出意见，拟同意的，报国务院宗教事务部门审批。

国务院宗教事务部门应当自收到在宗教活动场所外修建大型露天宗教造像报告之日起６０日内，作出批准或者不予批准的决定。

宗教团体、寺观教堂以外的组织以及个人不得修建大型露天宗教造像。

第二十五条 有关单位和个人在宗教活动场所内改建或者新建建筑物、设立商业服务网点、举办陈列展览、拍摄电影电视片，应当事先征得该宗教活动场所和所在地的县级以上地方人民政府宗教事务部门同意。

第二十六条 以宗教活动场所为主要游览内容的风景名胜区，其所在地的县级以上地方人民政府应当协调、处理宗教活动场所与园林、文物、旅游等方面的利益关系，维护宗教活动场所的合法权益。

以宗教活动场所为主要游览内容的风景名胜区的规划建设，应当与宗教活动场所的风格、环境相协调。

第四章 宗教教职人员

第二十七条 宗教教职人员经宗教团体认定，报县级以上人民政府宗教事务部门备案，可以从事宗教教务活动。

藏传佛教活佛传承继位，在佛教团体的指导下，依照宗教仪轨和历史定制办理，报设区的市级以上人民政府宗教事务部门或者设区的市级以上人民政府批准。天主教的主教由天主教的全国性宗教团体报国务院宗教事务部门备案。

第二十八条 宗教教职人员担任或者离任宗教活动场所主要教职，经本宗教的宗教团体同意后，报县级以上人民政府宗教事务部门备案。

第二十九条 宗教教职人员主持宗教活动、举行宗教仪式、从事宗教典籍整理、进行宗教文化研究等活动，受法律保护。

第五章 宗教财产

第三十条 宗教团体、宗教活动场所合法使用的土地，合法所有或者使用的房屋、构筑物、设施，以及其他合法财产、收益，受法律保护。

任何组织或者个人不得侵占、哄抢、私分、损毁或者非法查封、扣押、冻结、没收、处分宗教团体、宗教活动场所的合法财产，不得损毁宗教团体、宗教活动场所占有、使用的文物。

第三十一条 宗教团体、宗教活动场所所有的房屋和使用的土地，应当依法向县级以上地方人民政府房产、土地管理部门申请登记，领取所有权、使用权证书；产权变更的，应当及时办理变更手续。

土地管理部门在确定和变更宗教团体或者宗教活动场所土地使用权时，应当征求本级人民政府宗教事务部门的意见。

第三十二条 宗教活动场所用于宗教活动的房屋、构筑物及其附属的宗教教职人员生活用房不得转让、抵押或者作为实物投资。

第三十三条 因城市规划或者重点工程建设需要拆迁宗教团体或者宗教活动场所的房屋、构筑物的，拆迁人应当与该宗教团体或者宗教活动场所协商，并征求有关宗教事务部门的意见。经各方协商同意拆迁的，拆迁人应当对被拆迁的房屋、构筑物予以重建，或者根据国家有关规定，按照被拆迁房屋、构筑物的市场评估价格予以补偿。

第三十四条 宗教团体、宗教活动场所可以依法兴办社会公益事业，所获收益以及其他合法收入应当纳入财务、会计管理，用于与该宗教团体或者宗教活动场所宗旨相符的活动以及社会公益事业。

第三十五条 宗教团体、宗教活动场所可以按照国家有关规定接受境内外组织和个人的捐赠，用于与该宗教团体、宗教活动场所宗旨相符的活动。

第三十六条 宗教团体、宗教活动场所应当执行国家的财务、会计、税收管理制度，按照国家有关税收的规定享受税收减免优惠。

宗教团体、宗教活动场所应当向所在地的县级以上人民政府宗教事务部门报告财务收支情况和接受、使用捐赠情况，并以适当方式向信教公民公布。

第三十七条 宗教团体、宗教活动场所注销或者终止的，应当进行财产清算，清算后的剩余财产应当用于与该宗教团体或者宗教活动场所宗旨相符的事业。

第六章 法律责任

第三十八条 国家工作人员在宗教事务管理工作中滥用职权、玩忽职守、徇私舞弊，构成犯罪的，依法追究刑事责任；尚不构成犯罪的，依法给予行政处分。

第三十九条 强制公民信仰宗教或者不信仰宗教，或者干扰宗教团体、宗教活动场所正常的宗教活动的，由宗教事务部门责令改正；有违反治安管理行为的，依法给予治安管理处罚。

侵犯宗教团体、宗教活动场所和信教公民合法权益的，依法承担民事责任；构成犯罪的，依法追究刑事责任。

第四十条 利用宗教进行危害国家安全、公共安全，侵犯公民人身权利、民主权利，妨害社会管理秩序，侵犯公私财产等违法活动，构成犯罪的，依法追究刑事责任；尚不构成犯罪的，由有关主管部门依法给予行政处罚；对公民、法人或者其他组织造成损失的，依法承担民事责任。

大型宗教活动过程中发生危害公共安全或者严重破坏社会秩序情况的，依照有关集会游行示威的法律、行政法规进行现场处置和处罚；主办的宗教团体、寺观教堂负有责任的，由登记管理机关撤销其登记。

擅自举行大型宗教活动的，由宗教事务部门责令停止活动；有违法所得的，没收违法所得，可以并处违法所得 1 倍以上 3 倍以下的罚款；其中，大型宗教活动是宗教团体、宗教活动场所擅自举办的，登记管理机关还可以责令该宗教团体、宗教活动场所撤换直接负责的主管人员。

第四十一条 宗教团体、宗教活动场所有下列行为之一的，由宗教事务部门责令改正；情节较重的，由登记管理机关责令该宗教团体、宗教活动场所撤换直接负责的主管人员；情节严重的，由登记管理机关撤销该宗教团体、宗教活动场所的登记；有非法财物的，予以没收：

（一）未按规定办理变更登记或者备案手续的；

（二）宗教活动场所违反本条例第十八条规定，未建立有关管理制度或者管理制度不符合要求的；

（三）宗教活动场所内发生重大事故、重大事件未及时报告，造成严重后果的；

（四）违反本条例第四条规定，违背宗教的独立自主自办原则的；

（五）违反国家有关规定接受境内外捐赠的；

（六）拒不接受登记管理机关依法实施的监督管理的。

第四十二条 涉及宗教内容的出版物有本条例第七条第二款禁止内容的，对相关责任单位及人员由有关主管部门依法给予行政处罚；构成犯罪的，依法追究刑事责任。

第四十三条 擅自设立宗教活动场所的，宗教活动场所已被撤销登记仍然进行宗教活动的，或者擅自设立宗教院校的，由宗教事务部门予以取缔，没收违法所得；有违法房屋、构筑物的，由建设主管部门依法处理；有违反治安管理行为的，依法给予治安管理处罚。

非宗教团体、非宗教活动场所组织、举行宗教活动，接受宗教性捐献的，由宗教事务部门责令停止活动；有违法所得的，没收违法所得；情节严重的，可以并处违法所得1倍以上3倍以下的罚款。

擅自组织信教公民到国外朝觐的，由宗教事务部门责令停止活动；有违法所得的，没收违法所得，可以并处违法所得1倍以上3倍以下的罚款。

第四十四条 违反本条例规定修建大型露天宗教造像的，由宗教事务部门责令停止施工，限期拆除；有违法所得的，没收违法所得。

第四十五条 宗教教职人员在宗教教务活动中违反法律、法规或者规章的，除依法追究有关的法律责任外，由宗教事务部门建议有关的宗教团体取消其宗教教职人员身份。

假冒宗教教职人员进行宗教活动的，由宗教事务部门责令停止活动；有违法所得的，没收违法所得；有违反治安管理行为的，依法给予治安管理处罚；构成犯罪的，依法追究刑事责任。

第四十六条 对宗教事务部门的具体行政行为不服的，可以依法申请行政复议；对行政复议决定不服的，可以依法提起行政诉讼。

第七章 附 则

第四十七条 内地与香港特别行政区、澳门特别行政区和台湾地区进行宗教交往，按照法律、行政法规和国家有关规定办理。

第四十八条 本条例自２００５年３月１日起施行。１９９４年１月３１日国务院发布的《宗教活动场所管理条例》同时废止。

新华网 2004 年 12 月 18 日

Source: http://www.china.org.cn/chinese/2004/Dec/732346.htm

Decree of the State Council of the People's Republic of China

No. 426

Regulations on Religious Affairs, adopted at the 57th Executive Meeting of the State Council on July 7, 2004, are hereby promulgated and shall become effective as of March 1, 2005.

Premier Wen Jiabao

November 30, 2004

Regulations on Religious Affairs

Chapter I. General Provisions

Article 1. These Regulations are formulated in accordance with the Constitution and relevant laws for the purposes of ensuring citizens' freedom of religious belief, maintaining harmony among and between religions, preserving social concord and regulating the administration of religious affairs.

Article 2. Citizens enjoy freedom of religious belief.

No organization or individual may compel citizens to believe in, or not to believe in, any religion; nor may they discriminate against citizens who believe in any religion (hereinafter referred to as religious citizens) or citizens who do not believe in any religion (hereinafter referred to as non-religious citizens).

Religious citizens and non-religious citizens shall respect each other and co-exist in harmony, and so shall citizens who believe in different religions.

Article 3. The State, in accordance with the law, protects normal religious activities, and safeguards the lawful rights and interests of religious bodies, sites for religious activities and religious citizens.

Religious bodies, sites for religious activities and religious citizens shall abide by the Constitution, laws, regulations and rules, and safeguard unification of the country, unity of all nationalities and stability of society.

No organization or individual may make use of religion to engage in activities that disrupt public order, impair health of citizens or interfere with the educational system of the State, or in other activities that harm State or public interests, or citizens' lawful rights and interests.

Article 4. All religions shall adhere to the principle of independence and self-governance. Religious bodies, sites for religious activities and religious affairs are not subject to any foreign domination.

Religious bodies, sites for religious activities and religious personnel may develop external exchange on the basis of friendship and equality; all other organizations or individuals shall not accept any religious conditions in external cooperation or exchange in economic, cultural or other fields.

Article 5. The religious affairs department of the people's government at or above the county level shall, in accordance with the law, exercise administration of religious affairs that involve State or public interests, and the other departments of the people's government at or above the county level shall, in accordance with the law, be responsible for the administration of relevant affairs within the limits of their respective functions and duties.

People's governments at various levels shall solicit the views of religious bodies, sites for religious activities and religious citizens, and coordinate the administration of religious affairs.

Chapter II. Religious Bodies

Article 6. The establishment, alteration, or cancellation of registration, of a religious body shall be registered in accordance with the provisions of the Regulations on Registration Administration of Associations.

The articles of association of a religious body shall comply with the relevant provisions of the Regulations on Registration Administration of Associations.

The activities carried out by a religious body in accordance with its articles of association are protected by law.

Article 7. A religious body may, in accordance with the relevant provisions of the State, compile and publish reference publications to be circulated within religious circles. Religious publications for public distribution shall be published in accordance with the relevant provisions of the State on publication administration.

Publications involving religious contents shall comply with the provisions of the Regulations on Publication Administration, and shall not contain the contents:

(1) which jeopardize the harmonious co-existence between religious and non-religious citizens;

(2) which jeopardize the harmony between different religions or within a religion;

(3) which discriminate against or insult religious or non-religious citizens;

(4) which propagate religious extremism; or

(5) which contravene the principle of independence and self-governance in respect of religions.

Article 8. For the establishment of an institute for religious education, an application shall be made by the national religious body to the religious affairs department of the State Council, or made by the religious body of the province, autonomous region or municipality directly under the Central Government to the religious affairs department of the people's government of the province, autonomous region or municipality directly under the Central Government of the place where such institute is to be located. The religious affairs department of the people's government of the province, autonomous region or municipality directly under the Central Government shall, within 30 days from the date of receipt of the application, put forward its views, and, if it agrees to the establishment, make a report to the religious affairs department of the State Council for examination and approval.

The religious affairs department of the State Council shall, within 60 days from the date of receipt of the application made by the national religious body or the report made by the religious affairs department of the people's government of the province, autonomous region or municipality directly under the Central Government on the establishment of the institute for religious education, make a decision of approval or disapproval.

Article 9. An institute for religious education to be established shall meet the following conditions:

(1) having clear and definite training objectives, a charter for school-running and a curriculum;

(2) having the source of students who meet the training requirements;

(3) having the necessary funds for school-running and stable financial sources;

(4) having the sites, facilities and equipment for teaching that are necessary for its tasks of teaching and school-running scale;

(5) having full-time leading members, qualified full-time teachers and an internal management organization; and

(6) being rationally distributed.

Article 10. In light of the need of the religion concerned, a national religious body may, in accordance with the relevant provisions, select and send people for religious studies abroad, or accept foreigners for religious studies in China.

Article 11. The making of hajj abroad by Chinese citizens who believe in Islam shall be organized by the national religious body of Islam.

Chapter III. Sites for Religious Activities

Article 12. Collective religious activities of religious citizens shall, in general, be held at registered sites for religious activities (i.e., Buddhist monasteries, Taoist temples, mosques, churches and other fixed premises for religious activities), organized by the sites for religious activities or religious bodies, and presided over by religious personnel or other persons who are qualified under the prescriptions of the religion concerned, and the process of such activities shall be in compliance with religious doctrines and canons.

Article 13. For the preparation for establishing a site for religious activities, an application shall be made by a religious body to the religious affairs department of the people's government at the county level of the place where such site is to be located. The religious affairs department of the people's government at the county level shall, within 30 days from the date of receipt of the application, make a report to the religious affairs department of the people's government at the level of a city divided into districts for examination and approval if it agrees to the establishment.

Within 30 days from the date of receipt of the report made by the religious affairs department of the people's government at the county level, the religious affairs department of the people's government at the level of a city divided into districts shall, if it agrees to the establishment of a Buddhist monastery, Taoist temple, mosque or church, put forward its views upon examination and verification and make a report to the religious affairs department of the people's government of the province, autonomous region or municipality directly under the Central Government for examination and approval; and for the establishment of other fixed premises for religious activities, it shall make a decision of approval or disapproval.

The religious affairs department of the people's government of the province, autonomous region or municipality directly under the Central Government shall, within 30 days from the date of receipt of the report made by the religious affairs department of the people's government at the level of a city divided into districts agreeing to the establishment of a Buddhist monastery, Taoist temple, mosque or church, make a decision of approval or disapproval.

A religious body may begin the preparatory work for establishing a site for religious activities only after the application for such establishment is approved.

Article 14. A site for religious activities to be established shall meet the following conditions:

(1) it is established for a purpose not in contravention of the provisions of Articles 3 and 4 of these Regulations;

(2) local religious citizens have a need to frequently carry out collective religious activities;

(3) there are religious personnel or other persons who are qualified under the prescriptions of the religion concerned to preside over the religious activities;

(4) there are the necessary funds; and

(5) it is rationally located without interfering with the normal production and livelihood of the neighboring units and residents.

Article 15. Upon approval of preparation for the establishment of a site for religious activities and completion of construction, an application shall be made for registration with the religious affairs department of the people's government at the county level of the place where such site is located. The religious affairs department of the people's government at the county level shall, within 30 days from the date of receipt of the application, examine the management organization, formulation of internal rules, and other aspects of such site, and, if the site meets the conditions for registration, register it and issue the Registration Certificate of the Site for Religious Activities.

Article 16. Where a site for religious activities merges with another one, divides itself, terminates, or changes any item registered, the formalities for alteration registration shall be gone through with the original registration administration department.

Article 17. A site for religious activities shall set up a management organization and exercise democratic management. Members of the management organization of the site for religious activities shall be recommended or elected upon democratic consultation, and then be reported to the registration administration department of such site for the record.

Article 18. A site for religious activities shall strengthen internal management, and, in accordance with the provisions of the relevant laws, regulations and rules, establish and improve the management systems for personnel, finance, accounting, security, fire control, cultural relics protection, sanitation, and epidemic prevention, etc., and accept the guidance, supervision and inspection by the relevant departments of the local people's government.

Article 19. The religious affairs department shall supervise and inspect the sites for religious activities in terms of their compliance with laws, regulations and rules, the development and implementation of management systems, the alteration of registered items, the conduction of religious activities and activities that involve foreign affairs. The sites for religious activities shall accept the supervision and inspection by the religious affairs department.

Article 20. A site for religious activities may accept donations from citizens in accordance with religious customs, but no means of compulsion or apportionment may be adopted.

No non-religious bodies or sites not for religious activities may organize or hold any religious activities, nor accept any religious donations.

Article 21. Religious articles, artworks and publications may be sold in the sites for religious activities.

A Buddhist monastery, Taoist temple, mosque or church that is registered as a site for religious activities (hereinafter referred to as a monastery, temple, mosque or church) may, in accordance with the relevant provisions of the State, compile and publish reference publications to be circulated within religious circles.

Article 22. Where a large-scale religious activity, in which different provinces, autonomous regions and municipalities directly under the Central Government are involved and which is beyond the accommodation capacity of a site for religious activities, is to be held, or where a large-scale religious activity is to be held outside a site for religious activities, the religious body, monastery, temple, mosque or church that sponsors such activity shall, 30 days before the activity is held, make an application to the religious affairs department of the people's government of the province, autonomous region or municipality directly under the Central Government of the place where such large-scale religious activity is to be held. The religious affairs department of the people's government of the province, autonomous region or municipality directly under the Central Government shall, within 15 days from the date of receipt of the application, make a decision of approval or disapproval.

A large-scale religious activity shall, as required in the written notification of approval, proceed in accordance with religious rites and rituals, without violating the relevant provisions of Articles 3 and 4 of these Regulations. The religious body, monastery, temple, mosque or church that sponsors such large-scale religious activity shall adopt effective measures to prevent against any accidents. The people's government of the township or town and the relevant departments of the local people's government at or above the county level of the place where such large-scale religious activity is to be held shall, within the limits of their respective functions and duties, exercise the necessary administration in order to ensure the safe and orderly progress of the large-scale religious activity.

Article 23. A site for religious activities shall prevent against the occurrence, within the site, of any major accident or event, such as breaking of religious taboos, which hurts religious feelings of religious citizens, disrupts the unity of all nationalities or impairs social stability.

When any accident or event mentioned in the preceding paragraph occurs, the site for religious activities in question shall, without delay, make a report to the religious affairs department of the people's government at the county level of the place where it is located.

Article 24. Where a religious body, monastery, temple, mosque or church intends to build a large-size outdoor religious statue outside the site for religious activities, the relevant religious body of the province, autonomous region or municipality directly under the Central Government shall make an application to the religious affairs department of the people's government of the province, autonomous region or municipality directly under the Central Government, which shall, within 30 days from the date of receipt of the application, put forward its views, and, if it agrees to the building of such statue, make a report to the religious affairs department of the State Council for examination and approval.

The religious affairs department of the State Council shall, within 60 days from the date of receipt of the report on building a large-size outdoor religious statue outside the site for religious activities, make a decision of approval or disapproval.

No organization or individual other than religious bodies, monasteries, temples, mosques and churches may build large-size outdoor religious statues.

Article 25. Where a unit or an individual intends to alter or construct buildings, set up commercial service centers, hold displays or exhibitions, or make films or television programs in a site for religious activities, it shall obtain in advance the consent of the site for religious activities in question and that of the religious affairs department of the local people's government at or above the county level of the place where such site is located.

Article 26. For a scenic spot or historic zone where a site for religious activities therein constitutes the main tourist attraction, the local people's government at or above the county level of the place where such spot or zone is located shall coordinate and deal with the interrelated interests between the site for religious activities and the park, relics, and tourism, and safeguard the lawful rights and interests of the site for religious activities.

The planning and construction of a scenic spot or historic zone where a site for religious activities constitutes the main tourist attraction shall be in harmony with the style and surroundings of such site.

Chapter IV. Religious Personnel

Article 27. Religious personnel who are determined qualified as such by a religious body and reported for the record to the religious affairs department of the people's government at or above the county level may engage in professional religious activities.

The succession of living Buddhas in Tibetan Buddhism shall be conducted under the guidance of Buddhist bodies and in accordance with the religious rites and rituals and historical conventions, and be reported for approval to the religious affairs department of the people's government at or above the level of a city divided into districts, or to the people's government at or above the level of a city divided into districts. With respect to Catholic bishops, the matter shall be reported for the record by the national religious body of the Catholic Church to the religious affairs department of the State Council.

Article 28. Where religious personnel are to assume or leave the chief religious posts of a site for religious activities, the matter shall, upon consent by the religious body of the religion concerned, be reported to the religious affairs department of the people's government at or above the county level for the record.

Article 29. The presiding over of religious activities, conduction of religious ceremonies, sorting out of religious scriptures and pursuit of religious and cultural research by religious personnel are protected by law.

Chapter V. Religious Property

Article 30. The land legally used by a religious body or a site for religious activities, the houses, structures and facilities legally owned or used by such body or site, and its other legal property and proceeds thereof, are protected by law.

No organization or individual may encroach upon, loot, privately divide up, damage, destroy, or, illegally seal up, impound, freeze, confiscate or dispose of the legal property of a religious body or a site for religious activities, nor damage or destroy cultural relics possessed or used by a religious body or a site for religious activities.

Article 31. The houses owned and the land used by a religious body or a site for religious activities shall, according to law, be registered with the real estate department and the land administration department of the local people's government at or above the county level, and be granted the certificate of ownership and the certificate of right to use; where the property right is altered, the formalities for alteration registration shall be gone through without delay.

The land administration department shall, when determining and altering the land-use right of a religious body or a site for religious activities, solicit the views of the religious affairs department of the people's government at the same level.

Article 32. The houses and structures used for religious activities by a site for religious activities, and their accessory houses for the daily use of religious personnel as well, shall not be transferred, mortgaged or used as investments in kind.

Article 33. Where the houses or structures of a religious body or a site for religious activities need to be demolished or relocated because of city planning or construction of key projects, the demolisher shall consult with the religious body or the site for religious activities concerned, and solicit the views of the relevant religious affairs department. If, after consultation, all the parties concerned agree to the demolition, the demolisher shall rebuild the houses or structures demolished, or, in accordance with the relevant provisions of the State, make compensation on the basis of the appraised market price of the houses or structures demolished.

Article 34. A religious body or a site for religious activities may operate public undertakings according to law, and the proceeds and other lawful income therefrom shall be subject to financial and accounting management, and be used for the activities that are commensurate with the purpose of the religious body or the site for religious activities, or for public undertakings.

Article 35. A religious body or a site for religious activities may, in accordance with the relevant provisions of the State, accept donations from organizations and individuals at home or abroad, which shall be used for the activities that are commensurate with the purpose of the religious body or the site for religious activities.

Article 36. A religious body or a site for religious activities shall implement the systems of the State for administration of financial and accounting affairs and taxation, and may enjoy the preferential treatment in terms of tax reduction or exemption in accordance with the relevant provisions of the State on taxation.

A religious body or a site for religious activities shall report to the religious affairs department of the people's government at or above the county level of the place where it is located on its income and expenditure, and on the acceptance and use of donations as well, and, in an appropriate way, make such information public to religious citizens.

Article 37. In case of cancellation of registration or termination of a religious body or a site for religious activities, the property thereof shall be liquidated and the property remaining after the liquidation shall be used for the undertakings that are commensurate with the purpose of the religious body or the site for religious activities.

Chapter VI. Legal Liability

Article 38. Where any State functionary, in administration of religious affairs, abuses his power, neglects his duty or commits illegalities for personal gain or by fraudulent means, and a crime is thus constituted, he shall be investigated for criminal liability according to law; if no crime is constituted, he shall be given an administrative sanction according to law.

Article 39. Where anyone compels citizens to believe in, or not to believe in, any religion, or interferes with the normal religious activities conducted by a religious body or a site for religious activities, the religious affairs department shall order it to make corrections; if such act constitutes a violation of public security administration, it shall be given an administrative penalty for public security according to law.

Where anyone infringes upon the lawful rights and interests of a religious body, a site for religious activities or a religious citizen, it shall assume civil liability according to law; if a crime is constituted, it shall be investigated for criminal liability according to law.

Article 40. Where anyone makes use of religion to engage in such illegal activities as endanger State or public security, infringe upon citizens' right of the person and democratic rights, obstruct the administration of public order, or encroach upon public or private property, and a crime is thus constituted, it shall be investigated for criminal liability according to law; if no crime is constituted, the relevant competent department shall give it an administrative penalty according to law; if any loss is caused to a citizen, legal person or any other organization, it shall assume civil liability according to law.

Where, in the course of a large-scale religious activity, there occurs any event endangering public security or seriously disrupting public order, the matter shall be handled on the spot and penalties shall be imposed in accordance with the laws and administrative regulations on assembly, procession and demonstration; if the religious body, monastery, temple, mosque or church that sponsors such large-scale religious activity is responsible therefor, the registration administration department shall cancel its registration.

Where anyone organizes a large-scale religious activity without approval, the religious affairs department shall order it to discontinue such activities and shall confiscate the illegal gains, if any; and it may concurrently impose thereupon a fine of not less than one time but not more than three times the illegal gains. In addition, if the large-scale religious activity is organized by a religious body or a site for religious activities without approval, the registration administration department may order the religious body or the site for religious activities to dismiss and replace the person-in-charge who is directly responsible therefor.

Article 41. Where a religious body or a site for religious activities commits any of the following acts, the religious affairs department shall order it to make corrections; if the circumstances are relatively serious, the registration administration department shall order the religious body or the site for religious activities to dismiss and replace the person-in-charge who is directly responsible therefor; if the circumstances are serious, the registration administration department shall cancel the registration of such religious body or site for religious activities and confiscate the unlawful property or things of value, if any:

(1) failing to go through the formalities for alteration registration or submission for the record in accordance with the relevant provisions;

(2) in the case of a site for religious activities, in violation of Article 18 of these Regulations, failing to formulate relevant management systems, or failing to have the management systems meet the requirements;

(3) failing to report, without delay, on the occurrence of any major accident or event in a site for religious activities, thus causing serious consequences;

(4) contravening the principle of independence and self-governance in violation of the provisions of Article 4 of these Regulations;

(5) accepting donations from home or abroad in violation of the provisions of the State; or

(6) refusing to accept supervision and administration conducted by the registration administration department according to law.

Article 42. Where any publications involving religious contents contain the contents prohibited by the second paragraph of Article 7 of these Regulations, the relevant competent department shall impose administrative penalties upon the relevant responsible units and persons according to law. If a crime is constituted, criminal liability shall be investigated according to law.

Article 43. Where a site for religious activities is established without approval, or a site originally for religious activities continues to carry out religious activities after its registration as such has been cancelled, or an institute for religious education is established without approval, the religious affairs department shall ban such site or institute and confiscate the illegal gains; the illegal houses or structures, if any, shall be disposed of by the competent construction department according to law. If any act in violation of public security administration is committed, an administrative penalty for public security shall be imposed according to law.

Where a non-religious body or a site not for religious activities organizes or holds religious activities or accepts religious donations, the religious affairs department shall order it to discontinue such activities and confiscate the illegal gains, if any; if the circumstances are serious, a fine of not less than one time but not more than three times the illegal gains may be imposed concurrently.

Where anyone organizes the making of hajj abroad for religious citizens without authorization, the religious affairs department shall order it to discontinue such activities and shall confiscate the illegal gains, if any; and it may concurrently impose a fine of not less than one time but not more than three times the illegal gains.

Article 44. Where, in violation of the provisions of these Regulations, anyone builds a large-size outdoor religious statue, the religious affairs department shall order it to discontinue the construction and to demolish the statue in a specified time limit; the illegal gains, if any, shall be confiscated.

Article 45. Where any religious personnel violate laws, regulations or rules in professional religious activities, the religious affairs department shall, in addition to having the legal liability investigated according to law, make a proposal to the religious body concerned to disqualify them as religious personnel.

Where anyone engages in professional religious activities by impersonating religious personnel, the religious affairs department shall order it to discontinue such activities and shall confiscate the illegal gains, if any; if any act in violation of public security administration is committed, an administrative penalty for public security shall be imposed thereupon according to law; if a crime is constituted, criminal liability shall be investigated according to law.

Article 46. Where anyone refuses to accept a specific administrative act taken by the religious affairs department, it may apply for administrative reconsideration according to law; if it refuses to accept the decision of the administrative reconsideration, it may institute an administrative lawsuit according to law.

Chapter VII. Supplementary Provisions

Article 47. The religious exchange between the Mainland and the Hong Kong Special Administrative Region, the Macao Special Administrative Region and Taiwan region shall be developed in accordance with laws, administrative regulations and the relevant provisions of the State.

Article 48. These Regulations shall become effective as of March 1, 2005. The Regulations on Administration of Sites for Religious Activities promulgated by the State Council on January 31, 1994 shall be repealed simultaneously.

English translation provided by the State Administration for Religious Affairs of the People's Republic of China.

Printed in the United States
26856LVS00001B/149-350